Views from the Side Mirror:

Essaying America

Robert M. Herzog

with a foreword by

Susan N. Herman

President, ACLU

First Edition October 2019

ISBN 978-0-578-57242-0

Table of Contents

Foreword

By Susan N. Herman
President, American Civil Liberties Union

I 've known Robert Herzog for more years — actually more decades — than either of us might like to count.

It's daunting to try to introduce a man I know so much about, and this collection of essays on such a wide variety of subjects, in just a few paragraphs. But Walt Whitman helps me know where to start: Robert Herzog contains multitudes.

In the time I've known Robert, he's been an entrepreneur: envisioning and giving reality to original business enterprises involving energy and the environment, media and technology, music and wine venues, and health care communications.

He's worked on innovative programs for New York City (as founding head of the City's first Energy Office), as an officer at JP Morgan Chase, and with a progressive teachers organization, Teachers Inc., a groundbreaking program prefiguring Teach for America with its emphasis on inclusive education.

He's been an athlete and explorer: skiing, white water rafting, and climbing some of the world's highest peaks (Kilimanjaro, Aconcagua). (Robert introduced me to rock climbing a number of years ago and I still can't believe that he persuaded me to voluntarily lean off a cliff backwards, trusting him and the gear he'd attached to me to keep me from falling a lot further than intended.)

He's been an oenophile, a gourmet, and a cosmopolitan, able to recount years later what wine he drank at what restaurant, from Amsterdam and Paris to Park City, Utah.

He's been an aesthete, appreciating and patronizing photographers, painters, and sculptors.

He's been a self-taught filmmaker, whose acclaimed first film showed at multiple film festivals from the Hamptons to Los Angeles. He's also been involved with various theatrical ventures, supporting cutting-edge playwrights and actors, even appearing in a production of South Pacific.

And on a more personal front, he's been a spectacularly devoted husband, father, grandfather, and friend: cherishing his warm and multifaceted relationship with his wonderful wife, Margot; escorting his grandchildren on an eye-opening trip to Europe; remaining close with friends he's treasured since childhood.

Of all his avocations, writing has always had a place of prominence. Robert has written novels, short stories, poetry, screenplays, and — represented in this collection —nonfiction. The essays here are the products of a bold and restless mind. They cover a range of topics as broad as Robert's range of pursuits, interests, and ideas. They include very personal accounts: conveying his reactions, as a downtown Manhattan resident, to the events of 9/11; riffing on two quirky and somewhat Herzog-like TV characters — The Fonz, and Seinfeld's Kramer. This collection also thoughtfully probes many other topics Robert offers as aspects of his portrait of today's America.

Robert M. Herzog

Robert's range of thoughts on the topics of our day is as individual as it is broad. He does not toe the line of any political party. He marches to his own ever-changing beat.

I am writing here as Robert's friend, but since I am also identified as President of the ACLU, I'll end by remarking that although Robert deeply values civil liberties, as an independent thinker he has not infrequently been known to challenge my positions and beliefs. Fortunately for our friendship, we civil libertarians believe that reasonable people can and do differ.

These essays speak for themselves, as the free speech of a very free and thoughtful speaker and writer.

San Francisco, May 2019

Stanley calls a little after nine in the morning.

"Turn on the TV," he says.

"Which channel?"

"Any channel. You won't believe what you're seeing."

Stanley's sense of wonder is not mine, I have no particular expectation, other than it would be some odd tidbit of human behavior he reveled in mocking, probably to do with the Mayoral election. Some Sharpton shenanigan.

On TV, the World Trade Center Towers are burning. Erupting black smoke and flame. A mile south of where I live.

I run to put in my contact lenses. The next day I will find usual objects in unusual places, not remembering how they got there. I grab binoculars, dash downstairs. I live at the corner of Washington and Charles Streets, ten blocks south of Fourteenth Street, a mile and change north of the World Trade Center. From there I have a straight view looking downtown, a familiar view of a street that didn't stretch into infinity but ended in a great glass and steel frame, so familiar I barely noticed it most days. Now the street ends in great plumes of smoke, an incomprehensible picture.

The street is full, barely known faces that are neighbors in a New York community. The air is full of explanation and exclamation. I look away a second, then back as a wave of screams and cries crashes up Washington Street, cars stop, people point, shouts, "Oh shit," young voices, Hispanic accents, everybody, people pointing. My mind can't process what my eyes see. I think it is just heavier smoke, further obscuring the south tower. Slowly I seem to see that only one tower still stands, but I keep looking for the other, a tongue gnawing at a cavity.

4

Red flames burn behind the gray/white steel girders of the remaining building, shreds of steel hanging like dead skin on the façade. I run upstairs, seeking on the TV a better understanding of what I had ostensibly witnessed. They play the collapse. What was unthinkable becomes inevitable. I run back downstairs. There is no doubt now. Watch as the second tower falls on itself, implodes. The crash smothers the flames, great black and gray and brown plumes shriek out around the tower. My mind holds them in place like after images. We can't see the bases, only the smoke filling the sky.

They are gone, just gone.

I wait a while longer, but oddly, there is now nothing to see from the street, except huge clouds that smother the skies to the south.

I go back upstairs, watch with the rest of the world. It is happening so close, yet in another world. I can no longer distinguish between what I saw directly and what I saw on TV, over and over. From where I stood, the crashes were silent, the ground steady, only the cries of people filled the air until it burst with wonder and horror.

These buildings were gone, just gone. How could that be?

This Really is a Crisis

Published as "Sowing Seeds of Self-destruction?
Nov. 3, 2002

> *When a war becomes chronic, it saps the vitality of a nation,*
> *and it will surely be lost.*

S ome 200 years after its founding, the United States faces one of the severest tests of its guiding principles and national character it has ever encountered. External circumstances and domestic personalities have combined to threaten the extraordinary experiment this nation represents. The history of empires should tell us we need to pay attention.

We need to stop feeding delusions of omnipotence and self-serving assumptions about our nation. Europe has had high speed trains for decades; ours crack after a few months. A single shooter creates a horrifying model of community disruption and costly breakdown. The land of the free has the highest incarceration rate in the world.

Our supposed great national wealth is confined to a few while an ever greater disparity of standard of living grows between rich and poor.

We can't afford to continue to believe in the inevitability of our power, that some divinely guided actions will insure we will prevail. For starters, we cannot win a war *on* something. It's hard enough to win a war *with* something, such as a nation. The "War" on drugs is a prime example. It has been a fruitless, costly and devastating exercise for years, yet it perseveres.

When a war becomes chronic, it saps the vitality of a nation, and it will surely be lost.

Compounding the crisis, we have an administration elected by a minority of Americans under shaky circumstances. A different breed of men would have reached out to bridge these gaps and carry forward the traditions of American democracy. Instead, those now in power appear like opportunists looking to get out of their stay in power what they can, while imposing on America a set of policies frozen in time — energy policy without conservation, foreign affairs without multi-lateralism.

A demonstrable majority of us didn't sign on for this. We don't want an administration that unilaterally guts longstanding international accords and domestic policies, such as in the environment, and destroys our credibility around the world, looking like the big bully in the schoolyard, maybe carrying the most candy now, but with a future doomed to failure.

Bush's foreign policy is arguably the best case for American isolationism, since it invariably leaves behind worse than what it starts. Americans aren't good at playing realpolitik, as demonstrated by Henry Kissinger. We support terrible people, creating long term hatreds that only come to haunt us. We hide oil-based commercial interests behind a thin veil of human rights that further erodes our credibility.

The "American street" is full of people of good will, genuinely concerned about the well-being of others. But so long as they are more or less left alone they don't dig too deeply into leadership policies, have the patience or cynicism to understand the role the country played in the creation of Saddam, the death squads of South America, the destruction of peoples under the banner of American care.

The world has changed. Years ago the four minute mile was a seemingly insurmountable barrier. When Roger Bannister broke it in 1954, others did so within months. Sept. 11 burst the gates of moderation, and the now regular bombings around the world testify to the loss of boundaries which will be difficult to restore.

The administration needs to turn down the heat, not ratchet it up. Over time, that leavening is the genius of American politics, able to accommodate an FDR and a Ronald Reagan in the same century, a Bill Clinton and a Newt Gingrich in the same decade. Iraq is a manufactured situation — let it play out without escalating rhetoric and threat.

End the nonsensical, ineffective and inappropriate war on drugs. Take those who are trained for intelligence, field work and covert operations and put them to work battling terrorism, truly protecting national security. In the process save billions of dollars, and generate many billions more by legalizing drugs and taxing them.

That in turn would also relieve law enforcement here and abroad of an impossible burden and enable it to concentrate on genuine threats to our communities and persons. Ten years from now do we still want to be fighting terrorism with the same effectiveness as we've dealt with drugs?

Repeal the tax cut which furthers the grotesque disparity between haves and have-nots. The nation's economy boomed under the old tax regimen; does anybody seriously believe changes were required?

If possible, earmark the monies that come in due to the repeal for innovative world peace programs.

Imagine how much housing and land a trillion dollars could buy in the Mid-East and other troubled spots, to provide genuine aid that roots out the seeds of despair and terrorism.

The irony is the people most consciously attempting to create an American imperium, after almost two centuries of genuine forbearance, are most likely to bring the downfall of American influence and power. They muzzle informed dissent, try to intimidate dissenters, seek the simplicity of authoritarian solutions in the face of increasingly complex social and economic forces. We are no more immune to such forces as we are to the power of gasoline to ignite and gunpowder to explode.

Great nations fail when they place keeping things the way they were over adapting to change. The administration, in its arrogant, archaic, and opportunistic approach to domestic and foreign affairs, is creating a deep sense of disaffection and alienation among countless Americans.

In the end, that sense of frustration and separation may be our final undoing.

My wife Margot had returned to her part time work uptown that morning, after a summer off. She's on the upper East Side, a long uptown and crosstown away from our West Village home. I keep calling, get cut off, finally I reach her. Come home, I say, come home now. Just a few calls, she says. Don't go down the East Side, I say, it's near the United Nations. I don't know where that comes from; have we all been implicitly trained for these kind of understandings? I wait for her, watch the screen, impatient to see more, impatient for her arrival. And the phone starts ringing. It doesn't stop.

About This Guy

March 2019

I am of two minds. Shakespeare never explained his characters, sought to underpin their ways with stories of their past. He never tried to provide an explanation for Macbeth, just gave us the guy in this moment.

On the other hand, when we read Plato's Dialogues in college, the professor would often point out that who was saying something was important in fully understanding what they were saying. The point of view informed on the viewpoint.

So, if you like your musings straight, skip the next part. If you'd prefer context, then read on:

As in Chinese astrology, what may have mattered more than the day of my birth was the year.

1946.

And the year of my graduating from college.

1968.

The nature of the way we observe and respond to the world is informed by our varying degrees of experience, inquisitiveness, and reflection. As a brilliant professor of political philosophy at my college said: in the end, all politics are personal.

Within the broad contours of those years are my particular path. I was just one day out of the Groundhog Day of infinite possibilities. You can see the other variations in the 70 million of my Baby Boomer cohorts, who range from the those formed by the Abby Hoffmans and Bob Dylans to the Bushes and Trump, from Cheech and Chong to Bill and Hillary, from the exuberance of Bruce Springsteen to the repugnance of Ken Starr. There's a lot in between, and in between that there's me.

The particulars of this path were shaped by a pretty terrific place to grow up in, Bay Ridge, Brooklyn (although my great friend from those days, and the editor of this volume, thinks I may have rose-colored glasses on when viewing it). This is not quite the Brooklyn of dese and dose. It was a polyglot of Syrian, Italian, Scandinavian, Greek, Lebanese... and then there was us, one of the few Jewish families within forty blocks.

I never got to ask my father why he moved there, because he died when I was eight. There! – another particular in the fermentation of the years. I remember being asked by a schoolmate, hey, I heard your father died, and running away. I was already cognizant that this path I was on was different, from the others around me. The first one with a father who died. A rare Jew in the 'hood.

I was also pretty smart. Reading Sir Arthur Eddington on Space, Time and Gravitation when I was 12. There was a time when I felt destined be a physicist, to uncover the elemental truths, to be an engineer of the universe. (Although much of my sense of humor, particularly the ironies that abound in astute societal observation, were shaped by MAD magazine. What, me worry?).

Then I met someone better than me in math. That was a shock to the system. Like the windup toy bumping into the wall, although it took a few years, I went in another direction. This will sound particularly whacko, but that direction was prodded by reading Nietzsche. He said that a fact only became truth when subjected to a human value system. This was around 1965 or 66 when I read that, and it affected my Sixties-shaped consciousness deeply. I would still be a seeker of universal truths, but they would be human truths, not abstract ones.

I should note that as with most of my encounters with institutions, I was a terrible student. When I was six, I refused to join the Cub Scouts, not wanting to wear a uniform. I've never gotten along well with the formed organization, the bureaucracy, the systems divorced from the people managing or using them. The only people lower than me in class standing at Williams had flunked out. Until the semester after I went to Outward Bound, discovering the glories of the outdoors, that have stayed with me forever since, with gratitude, and a slightly different sense of discipline, that got me to more than the 25% of classes I had previously attended, resulting in– to the Dean, shocking – my making Dean's list.

That search for truth stuff only gets you so far. It certainly didn't get me past the Vietnam War, and the imploding sensibility it thrust on my age cohort. It was the clear, apparent insanity of the enterprise, coupled with the percussive relentless intent of pursuing it by the powers that be, that began to crystallize the under-formed shapes of my political and cultural consciousness. There wasn't a Gandhian dialogue of thesis, antithesis and synthesis governing – let alone controlling — the nation. No, there was this dichotomy in the conversation, that engendered as much amazement in the loss of common sense and decency as it did fear for self and future.

Although there was enough of that fear that upon graduating I entered a program of teaching in so-called underserved communities that were "ripe for change" according to the precepts of the ex-Peace Corp folks who started the program. So right out of college I was bumped from my New England college and Brooklyn beds into living with a black family in the Al Smith Housing Project on Catherine Street in lower Manhattan.

Look, we weren't rich growing up, and my mother — about whom there aren't enough words here to convey her extraordinary graciousness and the love I ended up, when I became conscious of real love, feeling for her — my mother shielded me from what must have been the tough economic times that required her to return to work a year after my father died, and kept her there for the next thirty plus years. So I wasn't conscious of privation at any basic level. No, I didn't have a car, but I took my bar mitzvah money for the grand European trip the summer of my sophomore year. Our consumption was more than adequate, if not conspicuous, and I grew up with a group of mostly first generation kids more or less in the same circumstances.

But now I encountered people for whom the $20 fee to apply to a college was an issue, even a barrier. At first I thought hey, if you really wanted it, then you'd come up with the twenty. Then I saw that the twenty represented a limit, a form of opportunity cost for something else that might be more necessary.

I've always thought that we learn the most about the body parts that give us trouble. I had my first kidney stone attack when I was 18, so know a lot about that organ. Lately, I've started learning more about the knee (sigh!), and the stuff around it.

Back then, then, I hadn't learned much about the circumstances and problems of the black and Hispanic and Chinese lives that I now lived amongst. It was a soul opener, to see the impact of seemingly abstract policies of far away politicians on the lives in the street, in the projects, in the schools. I taught school for two years, and never met a kid who wasn't capable of learning, yet many would never learn. For me, the school system was genocidal, killing hundreds of thousands annually, a feeling of anguish I continue to revisit to this day.

And oh – I kept getting fired. Everything was so political in those days, charged with not just sharply conflicting views but a new found license to express them, in action. My first year, teaching third and fifth grade after crossing teacher union picket lines to support community control, I got fired because I didn't teach the way they wanted and it didn't work so well. The second year, rehired by the local school board to teach 8th and 9th grade social studies, I got fired because I didn't teach the way the powers that be wanted and it was terrifically successful. See what I mean about my relationship to institutions! (My junior high school was one of only two that walked out the day of the Kent State shootings).

The first presidential election I could vote in was Nixon–Humphrey – Humphrey because Bobby Kennedy, who I had worked for, was taken out of the picture, removing my pale shadow as well. The lingering stress of "what might have been" has stayed with me, and I suspect many of my generation, ever since. I'd lost a father, and then over time the father figures of my times. Another notch in the psyche, that sense of going it alone. I voted that year for Eldridge Cleaver, an articulate Black Panther running on the Peace and Freedom party, and he was then (not later) probably closer to my views of government and power, of the appropriate stances to racism, poverty and social injustice, as anyone else I've ever voted for.

Just this past year, after a New York primary, walking down the street with some friends, one of them said to the other, was there anybody you voted for who won? We all said no. There's been little representation of my views, and a large number of my fellow boomers, over the years. No wonder I hate paying taxes!.

So there you have it, or some of it. I was from early on feeling different, have always felt somewhat orthogonal to the world, sideways to its conventions and standard processes. It wasn't a single transformative radioactive spider bite, it formed and evolved over time. But always this underlying sensibility has remained, the sense of difference. Hence the perspective of many of these essays, and perhaps also an explanation of the compulsion to write them – to shake my nation by its shoulders to instill some common sense – granted my version of it – into the body (and soul) politic.

I should add some of these sentiments and experiences have found their way into my second, as yet unpublished novel, *Not Our Fathers' Dreams*, and I'd be happy to share that with you as well. All you have to do is whistle.

I go downstairs to buy bottled water in the deli. Already people are lining up to do the same. Carry a couple of bottles up. Hit by the odd understanding of place and situation, I rush back downstairs, buy the now three remaining water bottles, a pound of ham, eggs, milk, juice. I don't know what might be available, what might be cut off. Upstairs I fill pitchers with water.

Our son Stuart calls. He lives uptown, West Side. Talks of shutting all their windows, turning on the air conditioner to filter the air. I tell him he might want to think about stocking up on some essentials, for their two year old son, just in case. He says he doesn't want to go outside, that the people who could do this wouldn't stop at biological weapons. I have memories of a news report that Cipro was good against anthrax. We have some, to prevent traveler's diarrhea, but where?

The Myth of the Wall

March 2003

There's no wall that won't be breached...

T hroughout history societies have to various degrees sought
to shut out what they can't understand or control by
building walls. The Great Wall of China is a massive example,
but so is creating industrial parks or housing complexes in urban
areas surrounded by fences and barbed wire. Or a missile shield.

The desire is understandable – it's a mess out there, filled
with barbarians, wild tribes, people not like us, people gunning
for us, so the simplest solution is to shut them out. Simple,
straightforward, and repeatedly demonstrated not to work.
Walls are always breached, by human nature supported by
information and technology.

The Myth of the Wall is now operational in Iraq policy – go in,
take out the wild man, create a buffer zone of democracy and
freedom. Just like we did in Afghanistan. The patent absurdity is
evident to everyone except the Republican leadership, who want
a win now and don't care what the downstream consequences
might be. There's no wall that won't be breached, by whatever
the avenues of information and technology, military or
otherwise, that exist. Just ask the Germans about Normandy.

* * *

Speaking of myths: Republicans have clearly created and maintained the myth that they are good for business. In fact the party is not good for business, but for businessmen, and only a small fraction of those, the wealthiest who, driven by self-interest, keep the party's coffers full. While one percent benefit, another fifty percent or so are suckered into thinking that the party's looking out for them, seduced by a mean social agenda that cleverly speaks to their gnawing bitterness at not getting what they think they should be having, angry that they have to pay for what the see others getting for free. So they lash out in righteous indignation where they can – abortion, affirmative action, the ingested perception that pro-environment is bad for the economy – which all works well for those one percent, not for the other 50, let alone 99.

Still, the Republican attitude on the environment can be mystifying. Angering the world over the Kyoto accords, betraying some decades of progressive policy, is just for starters. The Party hails the greatness of U.S. ingenuity and economic power, but seems to balk at what would be an obvious role to exploit those qualities, to become the world leader in techniques that use less energy or develop alternative sources.

Recently there were stories of new LED lighting technology that would use a fraction of the energy of current lighting, be cheaper to make and run, and be of higher quality than current products. But at present pace it won't be ready for commercial introduction until 2007. That's billions of gallons of imported oil that could be avoided. One doubts that Cheney's build a power plant a week for twenty years energy policy took this, or any other efficiency or technology into account. Why doesn't the US put a tiny bit of that proposed expenditure into getting lower energy lighting a few years earlier, saving multiple hundreds of billions of dollars for all consumers, business and residential, while helping us kick the habit of foreign oil dependence that so skews our foreign policies. Hey Republicans, what's wrong with that?

Maybe we should buy Cheney some more shares of GE, so his enlightened self-interest might coincide with the country's. For only money can explain the Republican's environmental dogma.

And hey, Democrats, where are you? The Republicans at least have a working myth; good for business. The notion of the Democrats as being for the common man may bolster union get out the vote drives, but decades of failure in welfare, employment, education and drug policies have left the Democrats like empty shells with notion to fill their insides. No Democrat has forcefully articulated that running the government into the ground – Reagan, now Bush redux – through tax cuts raising the deficits (unproductive debt, since it produces far less jobs that private debt but swallows up the debt markets) and yes, running rough shod over states' rights and certainly state interests, is good for business, for anybody but the blessed 1%.

The Democrats have further failed to respond to understandable claims of whites who have been denied opportunity because of affirmative action programs. No interpretation of the American dream can justify such denial. But since affirmative action programs have provided more opportunity for people of color, and because the records indicate that once out of college the recipients of affirmative action do well, there needs to be an answer, one that lies in more opportunity, not trading places opportunity. But Democrats have shied away from the issue, leaving, like so many others, the public relations high ground to Republicans

Our street is blocked off. We look where the buildings had been, look at the smoke, trying to place their position among the ones we could see, orient ourselves to a guidepost no longer there, as if compasses no longer had a true north.

An ambulance streams by. I think it's on fire, trailing smoke. It doesn't make sense, that it would be driving, but what does? I see another with a similar plume, realize they are trailing the dust that has settled on them. A train of smoking vehicles extends as far south as I could follow, as it grew dark their flashing lights, reds and blues and whites, stretched out the night.

It is after midnight. Fifteen hours have gone by in a dull glaze of repeated visions that vexed plausibility. Multiple angles of planes plummeting dead on, without hesitation, slicing through the walls, the ubiquitous modern vision of home video, every moment and angle relentlessly captured. At first I thought the planes had been commandeered, rented even. When I learn they had been hijacked with people on them, my shock increases.

The weather is perfect. A breezy summer day, sunny and warm, usually embraced as a blessing, respite from the cold to come, evolves into an equally lovely night, the great NYC royal blue sky tinged over the Hudson with a red sunset and pink clouds.

It is all so beautiful, in three directions

Fonzie and Kramer

February 1996

> *We laughed with Fonz with respect, seeking to share his strength of character; we laugh at Kramer with the distancing gratitude that we are nothing like him.*

And then it hit me: Kramer is the Fonzie of the 90;'s. Now what does that say about the television-reflected perspective of their respective eras?

The Fonz was intrinsically cool, part of a milieu, awesomely effective and curiously vulnerable; Kramer is intrinsically funny, *sui generi*, totally inept and completely insensitive.

The Fonz lived by a code of honor and a sense of invincibility. Kramer exists without grounding and has a social impact of near invisibility.

The Fonz made pronouncements, and gave moral guidance. Kramer gives one liners and gasps of bewilderment.

We have moved from an era when common icons can stir a majority of US souls, to a pluralistic time when icons have been smashed and replaced by the fast sound bites of special interest fame. It is easier to recognize Kramer's mask of bewilderment than Fonz's uniform of clarity. The singular coherence of the black leather jacket has been transformed into just one of many minor statements of distinction, and distinction itself is around the edges, not the core. Fonzie could fight off outer space aliens not by getting around their superior powers but by evincing greater comparable powers of his own; he won through checkmate. Kramer cannot encounter a gay street tough without yielding completely; he lives by knocking the pieces off the board and running away. He has the insides of a chameleon made of putty,

We laughed with Fonz with respect, seeking to share his strength of character; we laugh at Kramer with the distancing gratitude that we are nothing like him. This is an era where public amusement is at other's expense; our joke tellers are not sharing dinner with us, but standing behind the bars of zoo cages, imprisoned for our amusement.

Let's talk about hair. The Fonz's hair hearkened to Elvis, to rock and roll cool, to hair that was meant to be taken seriously, to cap tight black James Dean eyebrows, an effect both seductive and threatening, culturally conditioned hints of sex and violence. Others wore their hair like the Fonz, or certainly wanted to; he just did it better. Kramer's hair rises like the uncontrolled curls of smoke from Cossack tents. No one wants hair like Kramer, has hair like Kramer; it is amusing because it sets him apart, not significant because of what it connotes or inspires.

Maybe someone as centrally funny as Kramer today has to be a composite of one-of-a-kind ingredients. Were he part of a recognizable group, he might be politically incorrect for mass presentation. What if he were recognizably Welsh and reneged on a bet? Clearly Jewish and kept some money? Black and with his special style engulfed a watermelon? Nope, none of that would do. He does funny things sitting all alone on the social/cultural landscape; that way no one can take offense.

Fonzie lived as a rebel with a cause; to carve out in his world a firmly established ethically based individual stand. Kramer exists without cause; jobless, he lives to avoid attempting anything that would put him in genuine conflict.

Now, both Fonzie and Kramer were successful with women. And it must be said that girls were often an appendage for the Fonz, there and gone with the snap of his fingers. But they were there, next to him, the relationships to be seen. Most of Kramer's women are off screen, more there to show their impact on him, nudging a mischievous meteor easily off course for a while, yet always returning to its essential orbit.

As much as anything, Fonzie was in control of his world. It often meant shutting out elements of it, to achieve primacy in his milieu, but nobody questioned his authority; thugs ran, parents listened, friends accepted, enemies acquiesced, women responded. Kramer has no control in the world no agency, in part because he never undertakes a quest of significance. He is the eternal itinerant, allowing us to laugh at him without taking him seriously, in part because we can live with him not taking himself seriously.

If we were to look inside and find a hollow core, and Kramer was to share in that look, any one of us and him would presumably be engulfed with sadness and pathos, a sense of empty lives and a meaningless existence. But we are forever spared any such glimpse, for Kramer is all facade that shields us from it. Inside Fonzie we would see the honed finely tuned instrument of a clock, elements in harmony supporting a common purpose. He lives as a well-defined individual in a chaotic world precisely because of the coherency of his internal structure. His was an era that promoted and respected such individuals, who made decisions and lived by their intrinsic sense of values. Kramer exists in a fragmented world by floating on each eddy, never holding fast to make an independent wave. He reflects an age where positions are taken based on reading polls, and combining real personality with a public presence is an invitation to personal annihilation.

  Who would you rather be? Who would you rather watch? If the answers are different, what does that say about our inner and outer worlds, and how we live in each?

We are living in a demilitarized – or is it desecularized? – zone, a land of limbo. A few blocks north of us 14th Street is shut off. Nothing around us is open. Margot went to get a newspaper this morning and had to wait in line at 18th Street. She had to show ID to get back in, to prove where she lived. In New York. In America. A few blocks south, Houston Street is shut off river to river. At West and Christopher Streets, people are lined up and applauding the trucks and cars as they drive south, shouting thank you, cheering, holding up signs blessing them and their endeavor. Doing the same for those heading out, carrying what we can only imagine. We live in a large cage, accessible only to people with credentials. The streets are virtually empty, stores and restaurants all closed. At D'Agostino's, the only vegetable available is celery.

The 60's meet the Sixties

June 2008
Talk given at my 40th Williams College reunion

"A vacant place in America permeated the room like God's mist before Passover, killing first born hopes."

I told a friend I was asked to speak to the class of '68 about the impact of 1968. Wow, he said, that's tough. Why? I asked. Because it will be hard to say something new. No problem, I said, they won't remember what they heard before anyway.

But I'll start with something I know you haven't heard before, because it's from an unpublished novel — mine — *Not Our Fathers' Dreams*. Its title is itself a commentary on today's topic, for did a generation ever have as much explaining to do to uncomprehending parents as ours?

It's 1968 — a June night in a small New England liberal arts college. The night before his graduation, something draws the protagonist, Fong, down to the TV room in the house basement. One of the few black kids in his class is huddled in front of the TV, where a chaos of images suddenly coheres, and the kid says — they shot Bobby Kennedy, he's going to die too.

27

It reminds Fong of many moments, of men like our fathers who are gone, and that he wanted these men, not these moments. But that wasn't a choice. He returns to his room, where his girlfriend is sleeping, smuggled in before parietal hours kicked in — not all the old days were good. He lies down but can't sleep. "A vacant place in America permeated the room like God's mist before Passover, killing first born hopes." The night his Sixties truly began.

There's the start of the impact of 1968 — it was a year that killed first born hopes. That set us adrift, looking for a different land, a different nation.

I recently heard a talk from Brian Greene, a leading string theorist, who said that in the long eternity of the universe, from its explosive beginnings to its quiescent future, that perhaps life itself is the aberration, the unusual state.

Aberration. I liked the sound of that. It resonated.

It led me to remember one of our class of '68's defining moments, perhaps our 10th of 15th reunion. It was a beautiful day, and there we were in the march of the alumni. We were, then as now, sandwiched between '63 and '73, our before and after. The whole parade, the marshals kept shouting at us: move it along, '68, keep moving, keep up, '68. When the march ended, and we were supposed to go inside Chapin hall for speeches and such, '68 balked. We stopped.

It was a beautiful day, we were catching up, elements which overwhelmed the institutional imperative to enter a dark hall and listen to others. The class before, '63, marched right in. The class after, '73 plowed through us, virtually lined up in sized places, all those investment bankers. '68 balked. Dare I say it, we wanted to do our own thing.

Of course, neither the era nor the impact of '68 was monolithic. There was that roughly half who responded to the times by trying to live a different kind of life, one which injected value questions and considerations into all its element. And the other half — who didn't get it, weren't interested, and are still pissed off about it. We can call them...Republicans.

And if Dick Cheney and George Bush embody that thwarted anger at a changing world, then there's Bill Clinton, to remind us that it's easy to confuse self-expression with self-indulgence. That confusion accounts in large measure for the bad rap we got then, which lingers in the air, you can hear whiffs of approbation in speeches from the years before — McCain — and the years after — Obama.

What disturbs them is that being an aberration gives us a different lens, a filter unlike theirs through which we perceive the world.

What perspective, then, do we carry with us from those days, and what do we do about it today? My view may surprise you - I think we should be angry. The before and after wouldn't expect anger as the emotion of the sixties — our age, not the era — but here we have arrived, the sixties meets the sixties. I don't think we should accept either the revisionist history of the nature of those days or the dismissal of the values we developed and sought to inculcate in our lives and the world around us.

We should be angry because anger is the opposite of complacency. In an era of billion dollar paydays co-existing with massive poverty, in a time when the seeming smooth surface of race relations smothers the deep divisions that fester underneath, surrounded by catastrophic failures of management — both public — Iraq, the environmental — and private — the auto industry, finance — who can have failed to be angry over the last few years?

In 1968 we thought could put an end to alienation, that we would integrate the personal and the public, with each venue informing positively on the other.

But — they kind of beat us down. For what response other than alienation can there have been, a feeling of helplessness as we watch an even grander legacy than our own, that of the nation itself, shredded by catastrophic blunders arising out of hubris, arrogance, greed and stupidity — and I don't just mean the Red Sox beating the Yankees.

Wasn't there a moment when you said, hey, my family, my work, my firm, my friends, I'll do the best I can with them, because what I care about, what I believe, my big votes just don't count, I'm a hanging chad on the ballot of significance.

Like perhaps any reasonable person entering this age, I'd prefer to shut it out, find my own way, schmooze with the kids and — god help us — grandkids.

But we shouldn't. Amazing as it is — we know things. We have lived through cycles, the stupidity that destroyed great enterprises and the imagination that created new ones. And with our lens of aberrational perspective, now more than ever we need to make sure we are heard — now, as then, not simply accept what's handed to us.

To give the legacy of '68 — not just that we gave different answers, but that we asked different questions — contemporary expression, a legacy that said, hey, humane values are important, in work, in parenting, in loving, and even in politics.

So, think of these last forty years not as a wilderness, but as a journey, creating a foundation, a connection between what was and what can be. But to do that, we need to be angry, enough to say... enough.

Of course — raise your hand if you've ever IM'd; SMS'd; chatted; set up an RSS, a Wiki, Podcasted. Stayed up past midnight! Get with it — don't take yourself out of the game.

Maybe we won't be called the greatest generation. I'd be okay with the wackiest — or the most annoying. Let's be angry, whether it's at your own still unmet aspirations, or at a nation squandering its resources and citizens.

What then is the impact of 1968? It is a legacy that asks us to honor the offspring of new and different hopes — to challenge power when it masquerades as authority, to pursue boutique self-expression that defies mass market uniformity, to speak and act for human values when those before and those after would rather plow right through us lined up in the conformity of sized places on their way to the dark spaces of officially designated destinies.

Move it along, '68. Keep it alive.

Like all major events in New York, this one is a sell-out. I waited on line at St. Vincent's yesterday, only to be told they ran out of equipment to take blood; today they are full up and requesting people schedule appointments next week and around the holidays. It is also hard to volunteer. I am ready to go down and dig, carry buckets, carry water, anything. I tromp to the Houston Street line.   I had heard, waiting at St. Vincent's, of a volunteer staging area at Greenwich and North Moore, but at every barricade am told they aren't letting people in. I call a number, leave my name. Never hear back.

I wonder if we could even get out of town. I call around, what's the name of the bridge at the north of Manhattan? who operates it? is it open?   Suddenly I seem to know nothing that's essential.

Robert M. Herzog

The Wounded

We waited for the wounded, but the wounded never came,

Crushed, buried, not forgotten, now we search for who to blame.

We walk as if we're wounded but we know there is no shame,

We wait to join the wounded where the world will be the same.

They went up in the skies to laugh and work and play,

They went up separate lives, they did it every day,

Three thousand joined forever enshrouded by grief's dark gown

They went up in the skies but they never will come down.

We have joined the wounded, for no one a disgrace

Parts of us were crumbled into that ghastly space.

Our vision plunders skies in search of missing towers

But we can't restore the lost despite our greatest powers.

Grief's shadows vest on streets so suddenly undone

Clouds stranded in the skies forever since the day of nine-one-one.

Standing across the street from St. Vincent's hospital, where the ambulances and people were lined up. And no one came.

Everything happens for a reason.

No.

Everything happens.

Conversations become strings, passed from one friend to the next, incorporating TV commentary and information, on topics so far out of our norms as to be unrecognizable. Serial conversations about new topics; we are learning with the focus of children, confronted with a new problem. Will we now embark on a course that will define the rest of our middle-aged lives? There's no way to keep up or vet every voiced threat; we'll end up jailing the kindergartners along with the villains. It's hard to see happy endings, but the compulsion to take swift and devastating action is overwhelming. Will the country look in the universe's mirror and not recognize itself? Resolve is a balm for sadness, but it is not a cure. I keep asking, but no one knows what Taliban means.

The Failure of Human Organization

June 2010

How is it we have evolved with extraordinary complexity, to malfunction with such consistent frequency?

A long time ago, the strongest guy got the most meat and the prime spot in the cave. Most societies since then have formed around those principles. So much for evolution. No wonder scientists talk about sensitivity to initial conditions.

Back when it was spears or rifles and dispersed, relatively independent populations, the damage one person or group could inflict on the other was containable. Now, however, the consequences of our disasters are growing proportionately faster than our abilities to mitigate them.

Whether it's mullahs or dictators, financial schemers or immoral corporations, the scale of hurt and pain that can be inflicted on humanity across borders and continents is leading towards unsustainability for the human species and the social and political fabrics they create to keep them functioning.

We won't need a giant asteroid for the next mass species wipe-out — we'll be able to do that ourselves. Extrapolate a curve— the number of mankind-caused deaths over the past three centuries. The numbers are measured by the thousands to the millions to the tens of millions. Think what's next on that curve, for this century.

But we get stuck in the small pits, in the machinations of Palin, the woes of Obama, the surges and counters, the strife of Republican vs. Democrat, or the Saints and the Colts.

If we managed to sit a little higher in the arena, we might start asking some larger questions: why are people hungry when there is so much food? Why are people poor when there are so many resources? Why are people ill when we can produce so much medicine? More: why do people kill others and forego their common human heritage? Why do they hate when love would be so much more satisfying? Why do they divide when unity would be so much more productive?

Why are human organizations failing? How is it we have evolved with extraordinary complexity, to malfunction with such consistent frequency? Do we concede that such failures are the natural offspring of human nature, somehow embedded in our genetic code to play out dysfunctional programs over and over, just using different methods? Or does humankind have other choices, and are they still available to us?

Look at our national budgeting process. We constantly run short, and what's the first thing that gets cut — education. As a society we cannot organize to educate properly the vast majority of our citizens. The failure is fundamental and colossal. What do we do about it? Nothing. Year after year we all witness the same charades of hand wringing and fate-bemoaning, and then we experience the same thing over and over.

The overwhelming majority of our planet's over six billion live in societies which present internal and external failures of enormous magnitude. Driven in all such instances by them that's got, while punishing them that don't. Whether it's the phenomenon of hedge fund billionaires residing next to the homeless and uninsured, or mullahs driving their adherents to murderous frenzy to impose the power of their religious view, society upon society express incapacity to organize around what one might assume were fundamental principles that are the very reasons people form society, city, nation and belief in the first place — provide people food and medicine, homes and clothes, let them live in security and the opportunity to be productive through work, comfortable at home, and to find self-expression and community that satisfy.

We need to confront certain basic questions, and find new answers to them:

How do we build identity without promoting prejudice? In a vast world, people need smaller cohorts to feel comfortable, and experience dangerous anxiety when that sense of self is undercut, by change, by different values. How can we enjoy different food, language, and culture without wanting to stifle other beliefs?

How do we encourage the vitality of wealth creation while abolishing horribly inequitable distribution? We assume that to produce value means you want to keep all of it. But we were founded with the notion of the common-wealth, that there is a benefit to each in providing the foundations of security and happiness to all.

How do we allow for civil authority that does not become abusive power? The ease with which our recent administrations have run roughshod over due process, in the prosecution of war and curtailing individual liberties, indicate how fragile even our democracy is. If you wonder why ordinary Germans tolerated Nazism, ask yourself what have you done since finding out about torture in Guantanamo.

We produce organizations whose leaders by their very nature seek more, and both the people next door and the people who follow them suffer for it. So why think now there's hope for change, when all the variation in means and technology have just led to ever more destructive expressions of the human psyche? Perhaps there is no good reason — other than that, with the phenomenal tools of observation and communication developed just in the last decades, we know where suffering and hardship exist, where murder occurs, but we also know where resources lie, where redress can be found. The means to solve problems of hunger, illness and poverty amply exist — it is the commonality of will that is missing.

That will is misguided by the legacies of discrimination, prejudice, greed and arrogance that constantly confound the impulse to do good. The legacies of tribal feuds that erupt when they are not suppressed, from Yugoslavia to Rwanda. The upbringing that once had cute pony-tailed eight year old white girls screaming racial hatred at black kids just trying to walk to school. Or that propels our so-called representatives to perpetuate health and welfare policies of callous, indifferent destruction. Around the globe leaders steal life from the led, behind the convenient masks of identity, religion and the power that others allow to accrue to wealth.

The issue isn't which economic system works better; they have all failed. Nor which religion is true; they all have rationalizations to depersonalize the "other". The issue is why so many of good will, reasonable desires and decent instincts are thwarted by the insane who promote murder and deprivation to maintain their power. If we can't start getting answers to these questions soon, we may be on in irrevocable path where the disasters we can create will overwhelm us.

In the evening I walk to the edge of the restraining line at Pier 40, again try to get down, can only leave my name and numbers. I am thanked, it is sincere and polite, but feel like the wall of authority has descended and with the best of intentions is dismissing me. Strangers who happen to have a form of uniform can witness this carnage to my house, while I am excluded. I watch the plumes of smoke, seeking messages of hope. The smoke moves east, as if brushed away under Liberty's outstretched arm.

We Need a New Party

Dec. 2010

There is everything in the Constitution to suggest the Founding Fathers would abhor the current hollow reverence for their words that abuses their spirit.

From Katrina to the Gulf Oil Spill, from Iraq to Afghanistan, from savings and loan failures to the subprime mortgage collapse, we live with failures, repetitive, devastatingly costly failures.

If the Republicans and Democrats were waiters, we'd send our food back for lousy service; instead we swallow hard because it's all we've got — and let them dictate the amount of our tip!

Our core political institutions have failed us. They have failed repeatedly, for many years, and they are failing us now. We need a genuine new political party. Not a counter to the Tea Party, which is essentially a lightning rod of dissatisfaction. No, we need a party that believes in government as a key component of an orderly, safe, functioning society, and is willing to engage to make that government as good as it can be.

We cannot allow the enormous discrepancy between rich and poor to continue to grow. On the other, we must demand that government be ruthlessly more efficient in performing its basic functions. Without a synthesis incorporating these great elements, we are moving inexorably toward societal failure.

We need a new party because the current parties play to what separates us, and encourage us to define our interests narrowly. Faced with ideologies without heart or mind, the country is in danger of losing its soul. We need a new party to generate realistic solutions and recapture a sense of national identity and pride.

We wouldn't need a new party if the existing ones had bothered to keep faith with their own purported ideologies. The two major parties have become too constrained by outdated approaches and self-serving practitioners to be of any use to the country any longer.

We need the Buffalo Party.

Why the Buffalo? The buffalo is a uniquely American icon, in the flesh and as a symbol. When Indians killed a buffalo, they used every bit of it, eating the meat, working the hides for clothes, down to using the cartilage for bowstrings. Nothing went to waste, every part served a purpose. The buffalo stands for what we need a new party to stand for:

- <u>Strength</u> – the buffalo represents authority legitimately obtained, stemming from inherent strength and character, not power gained at someone else's expense or exercised arbitrarily

- <u>Limits</u> – the buffalo became nearly extinct because of the stupidity and shortsightedness of early settlers. It represents the tragic potential consequences of human activity

- <u>Hope</u> — the possibility of redemption from folly through effective policy intervention, which saved the buffalo from final extinction.

- <u>Conservation of Resources</u> – making the most of a scarce resource, reducing waste, accepting and adapting to the resource limits

- <u>Fiscal Sanity</u> – the buffalo was the back of a nickel when the nickel was worth something

- <u>AMERICA</u> – a powerful, home grown symbol of a mighty nation

The Buffalo Party's philosophy would be humanitarian pragmatism. It would be rooted in the success or failure of policies in achieving their goals, rather than whether they fit into ideological guidelines.

The Buffalo Party's Platform (for starters):

- We're not opposed to the wealthy being wealthy; we're opposed to the poor being poor. We seek tax, education and resource use policies that support that aim.

- We don't favor the rule of despots, terrorists or religious fanatics, but we do favor the rule of law. To abandon adherence to that rule is to invite degenerating into a tyranny that oppresses spirit and individual rights in the name of an abstract state that exists only to keep itself in existence, and those that rule it in power. Under those circumstances, we will cease to be a beacon to the world and instead become the intrusive glare of a policeman's flashlight.

- We are not opposed to businesses making profits, but are opposed to those profits earned at the expense of other important values. They cannot be gained by the easy paths of ignoring the environment, of ignoring the sanctity of individual investment, or ignoring the precepts of simple honesty.

- We do not believe Americans should do with less material goods, but rather believe that they can be created with the use of less non-renewable resources.

- We are concerned not because we are uncomfortable, but because we are too comfortable. The history of once great nations is testament to the cycle of rise and fall that appears inevitable. Think of the things we thought we would never see again that have occurred in the past decade – serious economic collapse, a global division among nations that threatens massive war, large scale slaughters around the world.

- Until our foreign policy consistently substitutes a diet of food for a diet of hate, we will not win these battles over the long term.

Obvious, repeated failures should lead to change. That they haven't is a testament to the political parties having achieved monopoly status by scaring us, that if we don't buy their product, we waste the value of our vote.

The Buffalo party represents hope for our future rooted in the true strengths of our history. It would be guided not by the polarizing, self-serving actions of both our current parties, but rather by a clear-headed approach to problems unfettered by past obligations and constraints. Imagine the party convention, where from Bloomberg to Schwarzenegger there could be an open discussion of solving problems without fear of offending narrow constituencies.

There is nothing in the Constitution which demands we should have only two parties. There is everything in it to suggest the Founding Fathers would abhor the current hollow reverence for their words that abuses their spirit. With luck, competition would force changes in the existing parties, who like most beasts respond best when threatened.

We need to reduce the insolence of office, and bring instead a quality of service oriented to those served, not those doing the serving.

The Buffalo Party: it's time to enroll.

*At the barrier line, people try to talk their way into going all
the way downtown, to help. A couple of guys claim they are
EMT workers, have construction experience, live in New Jersey,
had been called by their local hotline to come in to join the
bucket brigades. They wear yamukkahs. Their story keeps
changing slightly, I sense they are adjusting what they say as
they go along. But there is no doubting their intention, to get
down, to help, with hands and backs and will, to help an area
that had to test faith, that God seemed to have forsaken. But
human faith grows inversely to the desperation around it. I
stand with them, figuring their story is better than mine, and if
they can get in, I will tag along. Finally I walk home. A
schoolbus full of men in work clothes, the orange vests of
construction workers, burly men, halts on the way south. A
dozen people quickly hold up to them water and sandwiches,
pass it through the windows. As the bus drives by, its interior
lights on, I can see the men as if in a movie, so determined,
passing the food and water around, standing, talking quietly,
whisked south toward hell.*

The Disaffected Majority

Nov. 2011

> *You can say that we enjoy great freedom in America. But the reason we can say what we want is because nobody in power is listening.*

TV never captured the density of the Occupy Wall Street neighborhood. One tent abutted the next through the whole area, with narrow passageways among them. Tents from Colman, Sierra Club, North Face — a campsite on a concrete slab. The backdrop was ironic — the under-construction buildings of the WTC site. There were easily two newspeople or photographers for every OWS inhabitant, a constant scramble for interviews of the actual denizens, attempting to make sense of why these people were there and what they represented.

I spoke with Amelia, who worked in Facilitation, one of fifty (!) working groups of the General Assembly, the loose core of this disparate planet. She was there to take back lessons to Occupy Bronx, where she lives. And David, nineteen years old between high school and a Buddhist Institute which he believes is his life's destiny. He was distributing flyers from the Structure Working Group to create a Spokes Council, groups built around particular concerns who gather to create consensus. We used to call this participatory democracy, not the most efficient way to get something done, but certainly highly inclusive.

And Mary, a middle-aged woman with an arts scene blog, not a camper but a visitor there to walk amongst people who finally express her frustration.

We've had names for implicit movements — the Silent Majority, the Moral Majority, the Soccer Moms. The OWS group is the tip of the Disaffected Majority, rising from the purposeful alienation induced by the powerful who are quite satisfied with the status quo, for all the smoke they blow around it. The OWSers call themselves the 99%, but many of the 99% are living like pods in the Matrix, unaware of the opiates that keep them in their place to enrich the 1% running the show.

You can say that we enjoy great freedom in America. But the reason we can say what we want is because nobody in power is listening.

The OWS conversations and the signs all expressed this disaffection, being fed up and wanting change. It boils up without a coherent agenda for OWS and its millions of potential supporters, and creates no impetus to participate in the political process to create influence.

What has become increasingly apparent, but took the OWSers to catch up to and articulate, is that our government officials, like most governments, are in power primarily to stay in power. Which means catering to their wealthiest or most powerful supporters. We've had decades of failure in ostensibly public needs — in education, the economy, health care, energy and the environment. (Is it ironic or pathetic that Texas, which probably produces more climate change deniers per capita than any other locale, is undergoing an historic drought?). But our Government, a permanent population, does nothing to structurally, permanently improve these problems.

Assume for a moment that a. they're not totally incompetent and b. the problems are not completely intractable. Then you must ask, what is it that they do accomplish? For if you truly want to understand politics and government, you shouldn't look at purported goals — you should examine who benefits from the actual outcome.

The answer shouts out — they keep themselves and their cohorts in power and in wealth. And they will keep doing so until like the last emperor the barbarians storm the gates and take over, with all the ugly consequences of such disruption. We no longer have representatives of the people, but rather representatives of the people who can buy the people.

If our democracy is going to work, then the OWS movement will need to trigger the involvement of the Disaffected Majority, until they become an Engaged Electorate.

With a coherent agenda and a focused political outlet, OWS and the Disaffected Majority could have an impact on the terrible structural imbalances afflicting America, that have driven the nation so far off the course of equal opportunity and equitable distribution. Such an agenda could revive a concerned society and create rational discourse and policies. It will take more than what has started, but started it has. Whether it will end up having impact is still unknown. We can just hope, or despair, or we can start doing something about it.

Our house starts to smell. Forgetting, I think we are burning something in the oven. No, it smells electrical. I check wiring. I sniff at the windows. It is coming from there, a hint, but sharp, bearing its terrible connection. Stuart calls, tells me the wind has turned north, that we are no longer to be spared. There is asbestos, they say, in the smoke, but it is only dangerous under long term exposure. I run through the house, shut all the windows, lock them to get the best seal. Turn on all the air conditioners, close the vents, on some theory I could create a positive pressure in the house to help keep outside air out. I think of the bathroom vent and its perpetual suction, a betrayer within my house. I find tissue, cover the vent.

How do we think of these things? What implicit training and messages have we been receiving? How dangerous was it to think I knew about such things, when most likely my threat response was immeasurably futile. I shut blinds for further insulation. A cord is tangled on phone wires, an innocent tangle that becomes ominous and frustrating, minutes to straighten them. One by one, I grab the filters out of the air conditioners, and vacuum them.

We are now a cocoon within a cocoon, further isolated, retreating, besieged. Scared.

The air seeps through, the TV burns on.

The Failure of Critical Thinking

June 2011

> *Barack Obama, a pol who kept the same people in charge of
> our financial system who destroyed millions with it in the
> first place.*

I keep trying to look at it from the other side; do that non-judgmental, open, learn-from-it-all thing. But how do you explain Sarah Palin? Arizona? The Republican Party on global warming? And I'm not, repeat that, a "liberal." Government, like business, if left unfettered has inevitable tendencies to inflict grievous injuries in service to itself.

To paraphrase *Cool Hand Luke* — What we have here is a failure of Critical Thinking. We've let bad education, the policies that support it, the forces that starve our schools and underpay our teachers, the practitioners who get paid to peddle it, come home to roost in so many American nests that they have no view to daylight. Bad education leaves people vulnerable to appeals to the saddest, angriest, most manipulable parts of their selves.

Doctors are murdered by people who profess to be pro-life. Pro-lifers easily send our nation's kids off to fight wars that kill other people, based on false evidence and lousy energy policy. Of the screaming supporters at anti-tax rallies, 98% of them would be better off with increased taxes for the wealthy, but they are led by their sad, hopeful noses to defy their own self-interest.

The people who exploit all this know what they're doing. That Republican Party's adamant ignorance is part of a thoroughly choreographed and orchestrated means to keep them in wealth. Deny global warming, get less regulation on polluters, make bigger profits. The failure of education is a parallel universe the Democrats swim in, letting unions kill voucher programs, for example. Sarah Palin sells... Sarah Palin.

John Boehner (Boner?) reveres the Constitution, so much so that he quotes it publicly. Except that he was actually quoting from the Declaration of Independence. Think about it.

Michelle Bachman has a law degree (from Oral Roberts University), and staunchly preaches the legacy of American Freedom through the Tea Party, whose name derives from the Revolutionary War. She pronounced how important the state was where the Shot Heard Round the World was fired — except she thought it was New Hampshire. She's a leader in shaping public opinion. Think about it.

George Bush on WMD. Cheney on coal and nuclear (really, Cheney on anything). Privatizing Medicare or social security, because people will be so well protected by private markets. Palin on Paul Revere (or on anything). Ending air quality regulations. Not allowing controls of automatic weapons. Creating frenzies on abortion, gay marriage, gun bearing — while doing nothing for home mortgagees. Think about it.

Starving government of revenues, so that increasing proportions of what it does take in go to entitlement programs that do nothing to create jobs, build infrastructure, create long term value appreciation. Reagan and Republicans historically increased national debt, but with far lower job creation stemming from their debt; Clinton and Democrats decreased it, and what they maintained had higher job productivity. But ask people which party is good for business. Think about it.

Many projected all their desire for change on Barack Obama, a pol who kept the same people in charge of our financial system who destroyed millions with it in the first place. Who keeps us in the same wars with the same horrendous, needless losses. Whose notion of leadership is to be a great arbiter, as if we cared more about process than outcome. Think about it.

We're undergoing a colossal failure of individual critical thinking in this country, which drives a breakdown systemically. It has led to colossal failures of management, public and private; we had to bail out the car and financial companies, but can't bail out of foreign wars based on false premises and terrible planning. It's a failure that's more than foolish, it's dangerous.

Think about it.

Leave town, most of those who call suggest, asking why not. We can't explain. It's our home, our city. I was born here. We are sewn into its fabric, its essentials, there are not boundaries between place and self, between mutual love and support. They will not drive us from here. If the city is hurting, we will help heal it. We will stay.

The God We Lost

May 2012

*To be clear, just because men can bench press a few more
pounds than women doesn't mean they have any more rights.*

It's that season, when people are always invoking my Name,
saying how I'm on their side, and then doing whatever the
hell they like. Meanwhile, I've been trying to leave signs
pointing to Me all over the place. That's right, I am the real god
(or maybe one of them — ha ha, got to keep you thinking,
something that can go out the window when you ponder god).
So, if you're looking for that thing that's bigger than you are,
god, earth consciousness, universal awareness — here I am.

Now that we're connected: look, you're all My Children, and
such, but really, where you get some of your ideas is almost
beyond Me.

Let Me start by clearing up something that's crept into your
whole "what god is about" notions that's way off. I'm god. I
created all of you. And you're all equally dear — or screwed up,
Truth be told — in My vision. You, the next door neighbor, the
guy around the block, across the states, elsewhere in the
nation, in all the other countries and continents. Every god-
loved one of you.

Do you think I would Create all of you and then start
Choosing favorites? What could you possibly have been
thinking when one group of you encounters another
and thinks they're less god-worthy?

That some child whose parents don't share your faith or
language or skin color could be abhorrent in My Eyes, and you
have to convert them to your way or I won't Embrace them —
hey, Jesus, isn't that ridiculous?

However you define your set of beliefs, get this into them, into
your head — there is no us or them when it comes to repping
god. Why would you encounter people different from you and
try to convert them, when if you really looked around, you'd see
that everything I've done — and let me tell you, it took a heaven
of lot longer than six days — is to celebrate diversity.

I get such a high out of all the ways you take your thoughts
and speech, your DNA, and give them expression. Just walk
down Times Square and see how different everyone is dressed.
Each morning each of you gets up, sifts through your clothes
to find a way to say, that's me. And it's all as different as those
snowflakes you keep going on about. Screw the snowflakes,
celebrate yourselves. God bless your souls. Trust me, He
does. She too.

So for starters, end all the fights and crap that says one version
of so-called worship is better than another. Christians, let the
natives alone. Muslims, stop dissing everyone else. Hey Jews,
you're great, just not uniquely Chosen. Let the people with lots
of gods alone. Don't you think I can get lonely? All of these are
expressions, projections of your inner hopes, fears and desires.
I get that, but ease up on the identity thing when it means you
think you're better and somebody else is worse. You're not.

Except if you're French, and it comes to food.

About worship, here's what I originally suggested, but it got drowned out in all the paperwork and pageantry. Never worship Me, or Whomever, the same way twice. End dogma, structure and ritual adherence to liturgy. If you believe in Me or some equally valid other Version, then by yourself or in groups get together and give fresh expression to your beliefs, what it means to your relationship to the world, to yourself and to others. i.e., think about it, don't just follow stale scripts that reinforce all that separates you from each other, written by fearful folks in tough times.

Now I really don't want to interfere too much. Made that Decision way back when and have stuck to it, tough as it's been sometimes. As noted, Love the diversity thing, and that means let it go where it may. But you could organize yourselves better, around the things that matter and give meaning, pleasure and joy to your lives.

How's this for an idea: stop all killing. Each murder, individual or societal, is a pin prick in My Universe and a downer in the heavenly sphere. People or nations — stop making the tools of death, stop giving them out to all comers, and stop organizing your economies so you end up selling them to others to kill each other and justify it in any way. It's not just business; it sucks. Just because they're not on your turf doesn't mean they don't diminish you and all humanity.

All the resources that go into killing could be a lot better used all over your maps. Isn't it crazy why you put so many people in jail, spend so much on war and death, that you end up killing arts programs in schools, or reducing the number of teachers so as to render a good education impossible, or don't provide —

hey, it's a choice, not something pre-ordained — your fellow god-adored humans the most basic provisions of water, food, health and safety. What in My name are you thinking? I sure didn't set those priorities, don't look up and try to pin them on Me. I would never had structured society to destroy big swaths of earth to produce gobs of energy — where's the god/humanity in these choice?

And to be clear, just because men can bench press a few more pounds than women doesn't mean they have any more rights. Women really are Created Equal. I know, the original nature in human nature was that the stronger imposed on the weaker. Evolve, people. While that explains why so many men create rules that treat women as inferior, or for that matter how people use money, armaments and — and this really pisses me off — religion to dominate others, it doesn't justify it. Let My People Be.

Also, I really don't care how you dress. Or for that matter what you eat. Don't you think I have better things to Ponder? Do you seriously think that tells Me more about your values and devotion than how you behave towards each other, towards my other fellow creatures? Why listen to the people who propound nonsense, when you have the profound gift of being able to think for yourself.

Human organization is failing to meet human needs. It's instead organized to meet abstract requirements of church, state and corporation. To exploit entities which create facades behind which the saddest parts of humanity lurk, allowing a few to grope for power, wealth and identity at the expense of others, without fear of consequences. Who put profit up there with the gods, and why do you let anybody get away with it? Allowing a handful to despoil the clean air and sparkling water I Made just for you. Or trade death for power. An insulated few are draining

My precious Earth from the rest of you. Think about it. Stop letting them get away with it.

You need to get your shit together, people, because — and you have to know how much this pains Me — if you don't you're really heading towards some very unhappy times. Not the end of times — who dreams this stuff up? gotta love 'em — but times you wish would end.

Bottom line: I gave you joy, orgasms, senses of beauty and love, touches of the divine, available to each and every one of you, and look what you're doing with all that. Is the way it is the way you would choose?

Hey I've gotta go, I've already spent way more time on this than I planned, it's just that things have gotten so meshuganah (maybe they're not Chosen, but you gotta love the poetry). Anyway, a bunch of the Others have a poker game going next universe over (ps, it has nothing to do with strings), and I love it when they go all in holding nothing but a few empty galaxies. I gotta tell you, nobody's got the hands I do. Thanks to you.

Stay in touch. Just don't go crazy over it.

The first sight in the morning is a Ramapo Valley ambulance, heading south on empty Washington Street. Where is Ramapo? We pass through the 14th Street checkpoint on our way to find a paper. I am amazed to see buses, cabs, cars, people walking the streets with purpose, shops and restaurants open. It's like going from black and white to color. Vehicles without flashing lights.

We walk back, stop in a restaurant, one of the few open here, for some breakfast. The waitress asks me if I want rye or white toast. I look at her for a second, and for the first time in my adult life in a restaurant say, "I don't care." Really, it's never happened before.

A Choice of Supremes

May, 2012

*It is grotesque to think of someone like Clarence Thomas
deciding anything for this country.*

H ere's a reason this boomer, while disappointed with a lot of
the Obama presidency, will vote for him: the thought of the
Supreme Court being populated by appointees of Reagan, Bush
and Romney for the rest of my life is appalling. As can be
summed up by two words: Clarence Thomas.

In the period known as the Sixties, from around 1966-75,
despite all the turmoil there was one comforting theme for
millions of Americans — no matter what the President and
Congress were up to, we could still rely on the Supreme Court to
do the right thing

You see where I'm going with this?

In the past couple of decades, we've had a President anointed
by cronies of his dad over the popular will and defying the state's
rights they pay lip service to; Congress has become dominated by
people who solely represent narrow special interests and have
abandoned any pretense of considering the common weal, and

now we have a Supreme Court that is simply an extension of that Republican ideology.

It is grotesque to think of someone like Clarence Thomas deciding anything for this country, sitting without asking questions, clearly having decided his vote before so much as reading a brief, with no regard for the Constitution other than to cite loyalty to it before ignoring it to extend a narrow, mean-spirited ideology which leaves civil and human rights to the whims of the wealthy he is dedicated to further enriching.

The Bushes and the Cheneys were outraged at the challenge to their authority and the status quo that stemmed from those Sixties years, and have steadily exacted their revenge, by fanatically devoting themselves to concentrating wealth. They've created discrepancies in wealth that make the raj and the caste system look like a moderate form of socialism. Despite anything he might have said in the debate, there's no reason to doubt that Romney will continue, indeed accelerate, this process.

Not coincidently we have seen a rise in fundamentalism, of people willing to kill in the name of freedom and life. We are enacting voting laws that restore Jim Crow apartheid. There is an assault on women as state legislators transform themselves into mullahs — they shouldn't worry about sharia, they're recreating it. Rich oil and gas interests will frack and tar-sand drill us to death faster than our increasingly unaffordable health care system can cure us. And very brave young men and women are sent to die in wars based on lies and lack of purpose.

Millions of Americans are appalled at what is taking place. Who can't believe that the promise of years ago has devolved into such ugly, despicable practices. But inherently reasonable people are not devoted to imposing their beliefs on others, so they are not going to organize as a counter movement to the horrors surrounding us. Instead, they try to carve out a world of work, family and friends where they can integrate their values without spending precious energy smashing against adamantine walls. And hope for lack of impingement.

We need to start thinking of how to protect ourselves, our families, our children, our environment, indeed our fundamental safety and human rights, from people all too willing to violate us.

There was a time when I would have said that means trying to organize to restore balance and integrity to the public space. I've written elsewhere about starting a third party at the local levels to begin installing a counterweight to the Tea Party plutocrats. I've expressed hope at the possibility that a true majority of Americans would like to provide: mortgage relief to the millions ripped off by predatory financial practices; health care to all children; policies that protect our air and water rather than enrich those wealthy enough to build big masks and inure themselves from the horrendous consequences of their indifference to any value other than profit.

But it's not happening.

I had hoped that Occupy Wall Street would be the grit around which a pearl of a new party would form. Instead the people with that energy steadfastly marginalize themselves with inchoate plans and no capacity to develop as a political force. And if it doesn't happen around them, how will it happen?

The Sixties generation is not a major political force per se, and young people today have never known a system of genuine democracy. They're experiencing the residue of stolen presidencies, stolen resources and stolen votes, and until it gets a lot worse, which this country has a way to avoid just enough to undercut mass movements for change, not much is going to happen to create a path to make things better. The decent folk are losing.

So I wonder, why should citizens in New York or Vermont or other relatively sane enclaves have to endure the repugnant consequences of Republican policies? Let's not concede the secession talk to Texas. Why sink energy into futile attempts to create dialogue, reason and hope, when Clarence Thomas is destined to decide your future? Avoiding Romney will help, but whoever wins, it's time for something different.

The phone rings. I don't recognize the name on caller ID. But the woman asks for me by name. I respond cautiously, ask who is this. I'm not the right Robert Herzog, after all. "But it's good to hear your voice, anyway," she says. I thank her.

Venality v. Haplessness: The Underlying Dialectic of American Politics

June 2016

You can almost see the cigars laughing.

A s the conventions and campaigns come in full swing, the ceaseless commentary couches our politics as a clash between conservative and liberal. But the two sides of the fundamental dynamics of our political environment for several decades are better captured as venality vs. haplessness.

The dynamics of venality vs. haplessness are well on display in the issues of guns and the Supreme Court. Republicans ignore both popular will and compelling logic in their refusal to allow any form of gun control. Theirs is a higher calling – the dollars and voters of the NRA.

Meanwhile Democrats fumble for any foothold or leverage, and continue to fail. A failure running parallel to their inability to enable a President to exercise a fundamental right and need of the nation, to nominate a Supreme Court Justice. While venality propels Republicans to block the process, in the hope for a future that maintains a Court steadfastly supporting their economic interests. If the situation were reversed, and Democrats were attempting political blackmail, the Republicans would put up a firestorm of protest.

A partisanship based on ideas and conflicting philosophies is a healthy part of the democratic dialectic. As Gandhi put it, no person or side has a monopoly on truth. There is thesis, antithesis, and synthesis. But venality brooks no such perception and haplessness produces no resolution.

History is shaped by both underlying trends and signal events. Ours has been molded by a confluence of the relinquishment of a sense of the common weal from the Republican Party and the structural havoc they have wrought, which neither hapless Democrats nor horrified citizens have been able to stop. The cries of pain that animate Trump and Sanders supporters and the unspoken millions who share that agony are results of decades of policies and programs that have systematically hurt many for the benefit of a few.

The seminal moments of how we got here are a mix of slow burns and hot moments. It is no accident that some people rise to leadership, and the mowing down of a generation's leaders, the Kennedys and King, left a void that lowered the bar. The tone Nixon set destroyed the opportunities for racial accommodation that had just begun when he took office. The Vietnam War highlighted the beginnings of catastrophic failures of American leadership and judgment that became the norm.

That became more critical when the 1994 midterm elections put into office a Congressional majority built around a shocking value system: that they no longer represented, or even needed to, the interests of the country as a whole. That instead they were in office to stay in office and enrich those who kept them in office, and that government for any other purpose was subject to attack.

In Shakespeare or in film noir, corruption festers into long term consequences. So it was that the 2000 election pounded big nails in the coffin of American liberty. We had a rigged election, plain and simple: a bunch of daddy's cronies installing the son into office. The stench of that corruption has been rotting us ever since. Imagine how different the world's headlines would have been if Gore had won; think of a world without the Iraq invasion, and the lies that became the commonplace vocabulary of public pronouncements, lies that have killed so many.

Despite the closeness of the election and the questions as to its outcome, the Bush people proceeded as if they had a mandate. While the Democrats, perhaps shocked that the nation's highest office could be stolen, retreated into a corner of their own making. Bush seeks a trillion dollars in wealth transfer through revised taxes, and the Democrats declare victory by saying they held it to $750 billion. You can almost see the cigars laughing.

It's commonplace now to reference horrendous failures of the George Bush Presidency, but doing so obscures how successful it was achieving its major priority — the concentration of wealth that will maintain an elite for decades to come.

One can only imagine the collective gasps that erupted with the announcement some decades ago that the US will be a majority non-white nation by 2050.

The White America Wagon Train had long enjoyed an unfettered grasping of American opportunities. They had taken land, built factories, created and exploited a mass market the like of which had never been seen.

And now they had to insure their offspring would retain what they had gotten.

The Bush years enriched companies and people within its circle, while exploiting the fears and phobias of the constituents it in theory (only) served. Relentless in obtaining and concentrating wealth, while Democrats watched with verbal dismay and tactical failure.

The irony is that the very people who have been so damaged by Republican policies regarding taxation, civil rights, the environment, and who for so long have been kept in the fold by calculated appeals to their fears — regarding the rights of women to their own bodies, of fantasies of power that identify them with their guns, and with the dream of holding on to being rich that has 99% of them voting against their own realistic interests for tax and social policies — are still turning to the same party that has destroyed them to try to make their lives better.

This underlying dynamic was perfectly embodied in the recent show *Confirmation*, about the Clarence Thomas hearings. The Republicans, whatever their personal feelings, lined up behind their president and were ruthless in pursuit of Thomas getting confirmed, regardless of any inconvenient facts that stood in the way.

The Democrats were inept in countering the assault, to the point that they were, for reasons that even watching the show remain obscure, intimidated into not putting a corroborating witness on the stand, one who had come to Washington and was left in the wings. The result: a nominee to the court who year in and year out has with silent efficiency delivered for them, from putting Bush II in power to allowing money to dominate the political landscape.

That relentless pursuit of power for its own sake and to further extremely narrow interests is well on display as Republicans fall into line to support Donald Trump, bending themselves into political pretzels to justify his shortcomings, his bigotry, woeful unpreparedness, repulsive temperament and pandering. For one thing, pandering has been the stock and trade of the party for a long time; for another, they have no moral compass from which to respond, having given any up any semblance of serving all a long time ago.

They line up behind him because they still see it's in their own best interests, and while onlookers think they are observing a train wreck, Paul Ryan & Co. are simply looking in a slightly distorting funhouse mirror reflecting their image more or less completely.

Social issues shape identity for enough people that they can be cynically manipulated by those whose interests are even simpler – money. The accumulation of wealth. The generational capacity to keep that wealth and the power it enables. There are days now that foster empathy for what some Germans must have felt with the impending rise of their Nazi party; we assume it can't happen here, as we watch it happen.

At the barrier line, people are lined up with small boxes, marked ASPCA. For their pets. Stranded in Battery Park City. Who could predict that? I don't want more input, but cannot turn the television off. I am not hungry, listless, anxious without definition. We will live with grief, be surrounded by it, embedded in it, for a time as shrouded as the smoke billowing forth from the impact crater. We will have to learn how to function with it, balance respecting it with continuing, allowing even the trivial to be restored in the elements of full lives.

Stories start to trickle in, of friends and friends of friends, and family. So many of them have to do with the pride in being in that place. A friend's daughter whose boyfriend had finally advanced to where he was making a presentation. On the 106th floor. Another friend's daughter whose girlfriend had proudly started a job with Amex. On the 101st floor. Floor numbers became equated with sentences, life or death. A visiting father attending a conference. Colleagues reported his heart failed him rushing down, slowing stairwell traffic. They tried to help. Firemen came, said you go down, we'll take him. The rest made it. The father and the fireman are gone.

Border Streets

A version of this was published on Dec. 15, 2012

*In the fruit and vegetable department, everything was gone —
except broccoli!*

We were inclined to treat the reports of Frankenstorm as yet again media hype. Still, enough seeped in that we thought we should at least stock up on some things, simply in case there were problems with deliveries to the stores. And a couple of D batteries for the flashlight.

In the supermarket, then, the afternoon before the storm. Stuff flying off the shelves, long lines, camaraderie with generally bemused people waiting to board the same lifeboat, not really thinking the ship was going to sink. In the fruit and vegetable department, everything was gone — except broccoli! Which proves that people would rather starve than eat broccoli.

We became glued to the TV set, watching the impending landfall and areas that were already hit. Until in short order: the lights dimmed (a voltage reduction?); the FIOS-based TV went off, rebooted back on, went off again, came back on — and then the lights went out. I was, not for the first time, amazed. All that talk of underground lines being protected, what was that about? My first thought was that I had planned to cook a steak we had bought that afternoon, to have something in case of, well, the power going off, but never quite got around to it. Damn.

I stood by the window watching, not really heavy rain, but wind truly howling. Started seeing the flashing reds and blues of police cars, then heard in the distance, coming closer, a bullhorn-growl saying, "Attention, residents of the Village, if you live on the ground or first floor, seek a higher level." wtf?!?! I couldn't see any water on the street. The flashing lights made their rounds. Margot finally said enough, go outside if you want to but stop with the window gazing.   I went outside.

Our hallway was filled with the families with kids, since there were still some battery-powered back up lights in it. People asked if I was going outside, and reported they'd heard of high waters nearby. I felt like they were wishing me godspeed on a journey.

I walked the block towards West Street, which runs next to the so-called Hudson River Park abutting the River itself. Around two thirds of the way down the block, I saw water on the street. I couldn't quite believe what I was seeing, but as I got closer, even in the dark, I could see an unbroken sea covering everything. I climbed on the low marble wall that surrounds the Richard Meier glass towers and multi-million dollar apartments that sit on West Street, with the water getting higher beneath me, crouching so that the wind gusts didn't blow me off. A few kids had done the same, and were alternately laughing/screaming and saying they really should get out of there.

Right in front of me there were cars completely submerged, just the curve of a hood to note they were there. Cars under water, a block from my house, in Manhattan, NYC, USA. Amazing. That's when it sunk in, this was different, this was serious, this wasn't a lark nor an interlude that would quickly pass.

The increasing wind convinced me to walk back. I went a block east, to Greenwich, and saw large trees cracked at their base or uprooted, big branches scattered. It seemed like a good time to retreat, and I went back, reporting to the hallway throng that yes there was indeed major flooding not far away. The kids had wide-eyes, but it was still more adventure than threat.

We found candles, powered flashlights, coped. We had running water, but I filled up the bathtub just in case. We were pleased that we had gotten in dinner before the lights went out. The land line still worked, and I made and received a few calls, saying that this time the hype was like the stopped clock right twice a day. We were fine, surely had enough to manage. It was mildly disconcerting, but we went to sleep thinking it would all be back on by morning, what with the underground lines and all. Only slightly daunted by one of the callers mentioning they'd heard something about an explosion at the Con Ed substation on 15th street.

Woke up to natural light. Margot walked uptown, and found a deli with coffee north of around 27th street. There was now no cell service, Internet connection, and the landline had gone dead, which really surprised me since I've been in storms that took out power but not the phone lines, which I thought were on a separate circuit. We walked north, looking for the telltale of traffic lights, green and red signals that all was normal on that corner.

Which took us to the general Post Office across from Madison Square Garden. No service, but they were open, and packed with people finding outlets and charging their phones. Oh brave new world. We found outlets, made calls, and then went looking for food.

The restaurants were like border bars along states with different drinking ages. Filled with the refugees of the powerless. We wandered around, found a terrible burger joint, refueled. Margot had the great idea that as Equinox members we could go to any club (we were recent converts), and with a working cell phone and connectivity we found the closest club that was functioning, at 43rd Street and Fifth Avenue. It too was packed with people charging their instruments of connectedness. I showered and indulged with a steam bath. The small room was full, eight guys in close quarters, and when someone asked how many people were without power, 7 raised their hands.

We went home and found we were hit by a strange lethargy, a feeling of disassociation with the world. And it was chilly. It took a conscious act of will to realize we were not far from the land of working traffic lights, so we mustered and headed uptown. I thought I had timed a viewing of Cloud Atlas on 68th Street just right, but the theater was closed, I assume lack of staff. Bummed, we headed down to 63rd Street and got tickets for a French flick with la Deneuve; if there was something moving, we were going to watch it. Had a very tasty merguez sausage at Épicerie Boulod nearby, still reeling from the normality of this uptown world past the border streets.

After the movie we went to Cafe Luxembourg, a comforting familiarity, and then a cab ride home. This storm was getting expensive! The ride downtown was weird, lights on and then south of around 34th street, all darkness, the driver approaching each intersection with a caution I both respected and found irritatingly slow. A few lit windows, but mostly dark.

In our house, there was a loud thrumming noise. I opened the window and saw lights on in one of the small carriage houses along Charles Lane. They were running a generator, and while I couldn't begrudge them the effort, the sound was disturbing one of the few virtues of the situation, an unusual peace and quiet respite from urban world. Luckily the sound didn't carry into our bedroom — what would I have done?

There was however another disturbance of the peace the following morning. Our FIOS box was beeping as loud as a smoke detector run amok. I assumed it was the battery, letting us know it was running low. For all the good it had done us — where were the services the battery was backing up. I didn't want to try to play around with removing it, nor engage in the deep tangle of wires behind the scenes of my TV. So I took a small blanket and wrapped the damn thing.

It was odd, feeling so disconnected when twenty blocks north was so normal. Every time I went to the bathroom I hit the light switch. I couldn't do any work, the refrigerator was starting to warm up, and it was time to go. We had spoken with our friends Arthur and Diana uptown, and while they had their daughters staying with them said we could all make do. We took that uncooked steak, all the perishable goodies from the frig and freezer, packed a light bag, and decamped north.

We stayed there for the next three days, enjoying warm water and a camp spirit of good food, wine and whiskey. Not working full throttle, but enough. Even in the little world of my company eCaring, everybody had been hit, as I learned when all the MIAs gradually found connectivity. One person had twelve feet of water in their house near Sandy Hook, not sure it would be salvageable, nor if his charming small town would ever come back. Another had an "uninvited tree" in their dining room, another had moved from Westchester to the Upper East Side, another was still without power but had found a cafe with Internet.

What I discovered is that catastrophe, like grief, is an organizing principle, a meta-filter that radically delineates what matters and what does not, tossing out so many elements of one's everyday life, work and play, in that overwhelming moment.

Con Ed had let the most prominent real estate in the world go dark for a week. They'd had an explosion, vividly flaring on YouTube, by having power on when the water hit, and being caught by surprise by an extra foot of surge, a testament to their planning skills.

So we finally heard power was back on Saturday, and came home. We were tired. We got the TV working, and "War of the Worlds" was just starting. Great, some fine escapist fare, we thought. Except that when all the lights went out and an angry crowd started pummeling the last car running, we changed the channels.

If only it was that easy with life.

*I dream I'm talking with a friend about his son. "Will is alright,"
he says. "He's just a little worried about your bloodied upstairs."*

The Legacy of the Sixties: Not What you Think

Nov. 2016 – Post-Election Night

Self-indulgence can successfully masquerade as self-expression, a conflating which has spilled over into much unfounded criticism of those who did not exploit others in their pursuit of themselves.

I t's intriguing but not surprising how often references to the 60s come up in assessments of contemporary issues — the lingering impact on our political focal points and divides, our senses of identity, the role of culture in material and political society. For indeed those years created the fault lines for the schisms in today's America.

As someone who lived through that era as it evolved, I'd like to address some of the myths and analyze the relevance of what in retrospect was an aberrational period in American history, nothing like what came before or after.

I'm not talking about the highlights — about Woodstock and Chicago, the Summer of Love that became married to the winter of our disillusion. They may capture some essences of the time, but hey, most of us didn't experience them first-hand, yet we lived our lives in the times that produced them.

Many on the far right tried then and continue now to denigrate this as an era of self-indulgence, so to start, let's talk about this notion of narcissism, as some pernicious trait of a self-absorbed cadre of childish changeniks — because it's the opposite of what is true.

For it was service that was a dominant element of the times, service to and for the causes of others. The tie-dyed shirts obscure the history of many who put their lives at risk, and some who lost them, for the civil rights movement that began the era, for the ongoing challenges to feckless power when it posed as delegated authority, and for the anti-war movement that defined the era until its end.

Granted, people like Bill Clinton, and Donald Trump remind us that self-indulgence can successfully masquerade as self-expression, a conflating which has spilled over into much unfounded criticism of those who did not exploit others in their pursuit of themselves.

I was a member of a group called The Teachers, Inc. (TTI), founded by former Peace Corps volunteers. (Get that? — Peace..... Volunteers.) A powerful element of the Peace Corps was answering the call to go to foreign place to help others — no self-interest involved — and then upon return to see the place that culture plays in shaping our sense of identity.,

The process led to an understanding that true American Exceptionalism was the ability to understand, accept and rejoice that there were other, equally valid, ways of doing things — not better or worse, just different — to end the cultural nearsightedness of the post-WWII era. Most profound of all was to learn that what we think of as political is in fact deeply personal. That's no easy lesson.

TTI was the domestic side of the Peace Corps, founded on the premise that it could have an impact on the education systems of communities in need of and ripe for change. Whether in Harlem or Two Bridges in Lower Manhattan, or racially mixed suburban communities such as Westbury, Long Island. As a 22-year old TTI teacher in 1968, I spent a summer living with a black family in a public housing project, the Al Smith Houses in lower Manhattan. I saw first-hand what it meant to live black and poor in America.

That summer I had the assumptions I had grown up with — about bread on the table, about discretionary dollars to see a movie or, more powerfully, to apply to a college — shaken to their core, and that revised sensibility remains with me to this day. In that I am not alone. From how these issues endure, I have become increasingly frustrated.

Coming of age in the sixties wasn't just about finding different answers, it was about asking different questions. Bobby Kennedy's famously quoting"to look at things as they could be and ask 'why not.'" To not accept the biases of a society that was materially rich for some — by whom I was surrounded — but to pursue ways that the bounties of both metaphysical freedom and material comfort could be shared by all.

Then there were those who went the other way.

Sons and daughters who were pissed off about the challenges to their daddies' world, the Bushes and the Cheneys, the tight-lipped generals willing to send other people's kids off to a meaningless war fought for abstract concepts that meant death to those sons and to foreigners we only knew as numbers in body counts.

They are the other legacy of the 60s, even if not viewed as such: the half of our generation that refused to accept what the other half sought and who, through their well-funded relentless zealotry to preserve power for their class and race, have ended up dominating our politics, by fanatically devoting themselves to concentrating wealth, succeeding to the point where the raj and the caste system now look like a moderate form of socialism.

Much, I should say, to our amazement.

When I look back at how I thought America would develop from my 25-year-old perch, I never dreamed this path. We thought we were on a path to racial equality; instead, economic gains have been scattered and the separations exacerbated. The only difference it seems is that today black kids getting shot are caught on camera, because surely they were being killed the same way then as now.

We genuinely respected the dignity of work, but we couldn't foresee the rapacious capacity of capital to move its manufacturing bases to the sources of cheapest labor, destroying the guts of a then growing, and more tolerant, American middle class that has been left hanging in the wind by political and economic leadership that forgot who they were, except when they manipulate them.

We really really thought we'd put an end to horrendous adventurous wars predicated on narrow hard-line perceptions of American interests. Instead they cleverly ended the draft, so middle-class moms stopped protesting the spilling of their children's blood, and left a so-called voluntary army of brave boys with few good choices and no one empowered to protest the waste.

Oh, there was one part of our society that did remain sacrosanct. We thought we could depend on the Supreme Court to be a fair and adamant arbiter of the best stuff America was made of. Our poli sci classes were filled with *Gideon's Trumpet* and *Roe v. Wade*, and we expected much more of the same. That belief ended with the 2000 vote count, and the stench of that corruption lingers like a fog over the very core of our purported democracy, into a court that has become an extension of a single party's interests, a devastating blow to checks and balances.

Yes, these sensibilities were idealistic, but here's the core of them — we tried to bring a set of human-based values to what we did and touched, in work and play, in music, art and politics, in engaging with other perspectives and values with respect. We birthed impactful feminism, spawned Earth Day and environmentalism, created a world that produced the Beatles and Bob Dylan, and landed a man on the moon when we thought that was a precursor to adding meaning to life on earth. We even witnessed the first Internet connection.

Yes, we had it lucky. As we grew from adolescence to teens, the country was at peace, with a prosperous and growing economy that could be appreciated by both post-war parents and the first generations of immigrants (yes, immigrants) who relished the opportunities, all of which were passed on to provide us a sense of security, a confidence powerful enough to challenge norms because of a faith in the future.

But then we had a generation of political, moral and cultural leaders assassinated. Leaders arise for reasons, and their sudden absence set us adrift, looking for a different land, a nation where better natures could survive.

What the sixties folks sought in thought and action was an end to alienation, through involvement, whether through the civil rights struggle, the anti-war movement, or popular culture, into a society where all of us could be connected to the positive values and joy that comes from living a life of self-expression while not judging the lives of those around us.

We've kind of lost that non-judgment thing.

Four decades later many of us now experience a feeling of helplessness as we watch an even grander legacy than our own, that of the nation itself, shredded by catastrophic blunders arising out of hubris, arrogance and greed.

So forgive us if we strive to overcome nausea and alienation with the election of a man who on every level — personal, public, and professional — is the opposite of the rules of society we sought to nurture, in an America we were confident was heading in a better direction, until this recent second Tuesday of November.

Maybe we lost. But please, don't blame the 60s for the miseries that confound us today. Because those of us lucky enough to have fully lived in that era retain one abiding characteristic, that keeps us involved, fighting not just for ourselves but for others, supporting the people and the causes of freedom and fair distribution.

We still have hope.

I am listening to dissident voices, and for the first time wonder not if they will be heard but if they will face reprisals. Flying flags is easy, but what if it becomes another outlet for existing prejudices and vile energies? I'm not religious, but if there was ever a brief opportunity for a genuine spiritual revitalization in this sprawling nation, this is it. More likely we will return to what was, and be patriotic proud of doing so.

We talk of failures of intelligence, many levels. A flight school with four Arab nationals asking instructions about large planes. Was payment in cash? A report mentions a Muslim radical in German prison giving a warning that specifically mentioned the World Trade Center. Known terrorists using their own names come through L.A.'s airport. And there's a bit too much relish embracing the need for a realpolitik in using unsavory – the favorite word – characters for obtaining information. The history of the CIA and FBI don't lend confidence. Is the problem of our intelligence community the absence of its own intelligence?

Federer and Ali, and Us

Jan. 2017

But if we could see past our fears, we would have noticed...

T he fifth set of the Federer-Nadal match reminded me of another greatest sporting event. The Muhammed Ali-George Foreman fight, which I saw live at Madison Square Garden.

You have to understand, people feared for Ali's life before this fight. He was adored, admired, an extraordinary career to that time, but seemingly past his prime. Foreman had been crushing powerful opponents in single rounds, dispatching them quickly with punishing, relentless blows.

So when Ali survived the first round, there was a collective sigh of relief, he was still alive, let alone standing up. The fear for him was real, palpable, as intense as mass love can be.

When Federer would in recent years fall behind, lose just so-close, it was unbearable. I'd leave the room, the TV, go off to breathe and recover. He has established strong attachments, with his grace and elegance, his amazing shot making, his dignity. Ali could float like a butterfly, sting like a bee; Rajah could take a backhand behind him and turn it into a passing shot that seemed to defy physics.

Around the fifth round, something began to become apparent that if our perceptions weren't so clouded with fearful expectations we might have seen sooner. Foreman would lumber around the ring, throwing his killer punches, but they were falling short of their mark, not by accident but by the design of genius, an athlete who with intellect and the improvisational skill born of thousands of rounds, had figured out the puzzle of a seemingly unbeatable opponent. And with less than a minute to go in those middle rounds, Ali would bounce in and score hits.

Death and redemption. Survive and somehow thrive. These great themes emerge. Like the '86 Mets in the sixth game of the World Series. It seemed over for Roger in the last set, quickly dropping a game, extending Nadal's seemingly unbreakable presence from the fourth set, down in the last count of the last round.

But if we could see past our fears, we would have noticed how hard it was becoming for Nadal to hold his serve, how clarified Federer's game had become. Nor more unforced errors, no more forehand betrayals. Nadal was punching hard, Federer was doing his rope-a-dope.

We didn't know that was what it was going to be called, when we first saw it unfold, something new in the game. But Ali knew, somehow, and by the time we realized the pattern, it was the eighth round, with a minute to go, and the dynamic shifted again, and this time, built on all the previous times, Foreman the invincible unbeatable went down.

Nobody is a fiercer competitor than Nadal, as we had seen in his five- set triumph over Dimitrov, time and again punching his way to winning. We admire it, the brute force of his game, but we don't love it the way we do the grace and elegance, the capacity to surprise, of the Alis, the Federers.

And so Roger came back, and Nadal's hat ran out of rabbits to hold his serve. Roger broke him and broke him again, he didn't have any more answers when Roger came off the ropes and knocked him down. It was exhilarating, surprising, the joy of coming back from the brink far greater and sweeter, if more nervewracking! than if the outcome was more easily attained.

Nadal and Foreman, Federer and Ali. Giants pummeling each other, carrying the rest of us on their shoulders to unexpected places of communal intensity.

After the fight, all of New York had people shouting in the streets for hours, Ali! Ali!, a collective cry of triumph and thanks, reflecting amazement and appreciation, that we had seen such a man in action.

After Federer's victory, it was 8am and we took a nap. Circumstances lacked the communal sense the Ali moment had produced. But it was full and warm and joyous just the same.

Already we talk about rebuilding, what to do with the site. We are, after all, New Yorkers. Build it higher, some say, fuck 'em. Find a place to remember the dead, but honor them most by living.

Unable to be alone any longer, we go to the White Horse, one of the few re-opened restaurants, for the comforts of a hamburger and a beer, and the sounds of people talking. But Hudson Street has few cars, and all of those are official, spraying us in the red white and blue reflections of their lights. Traffic moves on Hudson in both directions, as if we could no longer afford the luxury of one way.

My wife's family is Dutch, and calls from there are filled with concern and stunned amazement. I hear similar reports, that Italy is dumbfounded, parties and weddings cancelled, Germany silenced. For Europeans, there was always a sense that no matter what happened there, if they went over the top, they always had America to look to, for support, help, and as a safe haven. With that gone, what was left?

I am so sad that this wonderful experiment in freedom is itself imperiled.

The Start of Something Big

November 2016

What will you do when the stone is thrown through the window?

When I was a boy, my father took me to a ticker tape parade in Lower Manhattan honoring President Dwight D. Eisenhower. My tall father held me by the hand in the crowd, and as Ike drove by, he said, "That's President Eisenhower. He's a Republican. We're Democrats."

"What the difference, Daddy?" I asked.

And he said, "The Republicans are for the rich, and we're for the working man."

That's still true, but sadly the working man no longer knows it.

The Republicans have long capitalized on polarizing social issues to fashion majorities, particularly effective on the state level. The successes of "them liberals" on gay marriage, the affront to even question who should be able to hold an automatic weapon, the sense that them others were getting freebies in health care and anything else that we the working man had to pay for, aggregated into a blind anger that needed an easy conduit. That, combined with the tone-deaf response of Ms.

Clinton and her minions, that somehow a 55 year old mine worker would be retrained as a computer programmer, is absurd, especially at scale, drove them en masse to destroy their host.

What we've lost hasn't even begun to be tallied. The genius of America for over two centuries has been its ability to draw from the extreme back to the center, through sharp internal strife. Part of that capacity derived from the checks and balances of executive v. legislative branches, and the dignity and authority of an independent judiciary. Now the Supreme Court is an extension of a party line, as cemented in 2000 when they anointed a President and as they have helped concentrate wealth and power ever since.

I've been reading the Philip Kerr novels, *Berlin Noir*. It centers on a detective, starting in Berlin of the 1930's. He's a decent guy trying to do his job, and we see the unfolding of the corruption and horrors that evolve, piece by piece, around him, in a place that wasn't do different from many others before that.

So, the question we all have to ask ourselves is, what will you do when the stone is thrown through the window? When a symbol of hate is painted on the wall? When the house of the "other" worship is burned down? When there's a late night knock on the next door over by men in uniforms carrying guns who are only following orders? When the fear that the next knock could be on your door is overwhelming.

In the words of German Pastor Martin Niemöller as he witnessed the Nazis destruction of the world around them:

First they came for the Socialists, and I did not speak out—

Because I was not a Socialist.

Then they came for the Trade Unionists, and I did not speak out—

Because I was not a Trade Unionist.

Then they came for the Jews, and I did not speak out—

Because I was not a Jew.

Then they came for me—and there was no one left to speak for me.

Tuesday wasn't the worst night, Tuesday was the beginning. With no effective checks and balances, with the control of the uniforms and the guns in the hands of men with authoritarian instincts, when the small hopes for addressing climate change are pillaged by the oil and gas-backed men, when the men on the Supreme Court begin gutting women's rights, minority rights, voting rights, civil rights, when — the list can go on and on.

The threat is real. What will you, what will we, do? The time to prepare is now, before it's too late, and we perforce become ordinary Germans on the eve of Kristallnacht.

Things fall apart, as the poet said. The center cannot hold; mere anarchy is loosed upon the world. Right now, anarchy's looking good.

*During the memorial service, an Airborne Express person calls to ask if I still want a package delivered. They can't deliver it south of 14*th *Street, but can't hold on to it, they are overloaded. What would I like to do? For the first time in days I get angry at someone, when for days it seemed that personal irritation would be unseemly, a betrayal of the times. I tell her her timing is inappropriate. I haven't heard from my cousin since the attack, she says, I'm just doing my job. There's no solace to be found; I give her alternate information, and return to the service.*

The Tyranny of the Minority

Dec. 2017

*When the majority of popular votes for President, and the
collective voters in the states, are consistently overridden, it
brings into question the legitimacy of the governing, a gap that
is a recipe for authoritarianism or insurrection.*

S enators representing 118 million people voted in favor of the
tax bill. Senators representing 163 million people voted
against it. Nearly 60% of voters in our purported democracy
were disenfranchised, with seemingly no recourse.

In their anti-authoritarian zeal to protect the rights of states
against a central government, the Founders in their Constitution
perversely enabled the minority to trample on the rights and
interests of the majority. That tyranny is infecting all branches
of government, corrupting the egalitarian principles which
propelled our founding.

Minorities now control the executive and legislative branches of
government, and have preempted the judicial. Operating by
majority rule is a fraud when a majority of votes in the Senate and
the House are controlled by minority levels of representation. The
collective voice of the people has been disempowered.

This imposition of the minority didn't happen overnight. From the outset of the Republic, treating blacks as three fifths of a person for purposes of determining census counts and levels of representation enabled the slave holding states to wield influence disproportionate to the number of empowered voters in those states, a disparity which continues to this day through other, equally pernicious means.

Systemic voter suppression means that a vote in a state that denies the vote to many within its borders carries more weight than a vote in a state that provides equitable treatment of all voters. A thousand voters in an open state can be matched by nine hundred in a state that suppresses portions of their population, each vote thus worth 11% more than their neighbors'. Denying felons the right to vote further distorts outcomes, mostly in those same states.

A decades long relentless and ruthless campaign of gerrymandering has eliminated open elections in many districts. The AP has estimated at least 22 seats were captured by Republicans thanks to gerrymandered districts; in Utah, Salt Lake City Democrats are scattered among four surrounding districts that produce Republican majorities. The NYU School of Law Brennan Center for Justice calls this level of gerrymandering "a threat to our democracy."

The Senate was created at a time when the population ratio of the largest state to the smallest state was 13 to 1; today it is 65 to 1. That enormously greater disparity between the large and small states makes a mockery of the idea that all votes have equivalent stature.

The electoral college is another toxic remnant of the slave era constitution, when drastic compromises were made to unite the states at all costs. The college warps national outcomes and thwarts the will of the majority, further reinforcing the power of states whose actual voters are a suppressed proportion of their attributed population.

Twice in recent memory losers receiving a minority of the vote have become president. That the beneficiaries of this distortion have been men who have lied to the country to plunge us into unnecessary wars while concentrating wealth among their kin is no accident; those willing to use the tools of suppression are those who seek power and its fruits over common interests.

The Supreme Court lost any claim or vestige to integrity with the outcome of Bush v. Gore, and the steady stream of decision based solely on party affiliation, turning off millions who don't want to get involved in the farce.

These interlocking systems reinforce each other. As votes on taxes, gun controls and other issues have shown, legislatures now enable small groups of people to decimate the will and interests of the majority.

The history of societal organization is the history of aristocrats, warlords, theocrats, apartheidists, the inner "parties" of brown shirts and red banners. Those that have the most want to keep and add to it. Democracy was supposed to be the antidote to such ills, but ours is in the process of failing, while a majority of good will and intent watches confused and helpless. They still trust institutions that no longer protect them, as legacy beliefs blind them to that fundamental shift.

The assault by the minorities has taken its psychic toll. Zealots keep at it, while their ostensible foes want a broader life and set of values. Republicans venally pursue power and their own interests, while Democrats haplessly try for greater inclusion and compassion, which puts them at a disadvantage in these power struggles. The result has been a systemic alienation of people who at a certain point exit the public space to try to find lives that they find fulfilling, within the increasingly narrow space afforded them.

There's a huge difference between protecting minorities from discrimination, whether in the bathroom or voting booth, as guided by the Bill of Rights, and ignoring the will of the majority systemically at the national level. When the popular vote for President, and the collective voters in the states, are consistently overridden, it brings into question the legitimacy of the governing, a gap that is a recipe for disaster, either in the form of authoritarianism or insurrection.

How can the majority regain its appropriate status? We can wait, and hope, for court actions such as the recent one in North Carolina, but there's a long distance between that action and national equity. One other way would for states to hold referendums on the tax bill, establishing alternative mechanisms to restore equity. And on immigration, creating sane havens. And the environment, accepting and acting on the threat of climate change. As the votes aggregate they can be used to leverage compliance at the national level.

There is an America which is decent, committed to the humane values of treating all with dignity and respect, to open the genuine American dream of opportunity and equality to all who are willing to work to achieve it. That is the America of the majority, who must reassert themselves, overcoming exhaustion and frustration to take charge where they can, refusing to cooperate where they can't, stop supporting or allowing the policies and people that are anathema to their values.

Resistance is tough, but it need not be futile.

We walk carrying air masks, remnants from a spill of toxic solvents in our building a few weeks ago. I am alert for shifts in the wind, look at flags flying, as if I am an operative on unfamiliar streets.

For days, the words of "America" have sounded in my head. I protested against the war in Vietnam, have struggled against authoritarian impulses in this country, railed against easy military interventions. Margot asks me if I was twenty-four and war broke out over this, would I enlist? I think a second. I am not feeling pacific now. Yes, I answer, I would.

The Social Determinants of Political Health

March 2017

What the Constitution is often really about is what the Bible is all about.

T here are some new buzzwords making the healthcare industry rounds these days: "the social determinants of health." They represent a growing recognition that many factors affect a person's health beyond pure healthcare; their physical environment, their access to needed services, economic stability, community support.

You might want to say, "duh." But in any event, these factors are being given increasing, if still minimal, attention in the healthcare system.

We have another system in ill health: our political one. No need to repeat the litany of polarization, presumption and pretense that are confounding our floundering ship of state.

What we need is to consider not just where someone is on the red/blue, liberal/conservative spectrum, but what I would call the social determinants of political health. The other factors that can undermine or contribute to a well-functioning polity, which are too often ignored in the louder, more obvious battles surrounding us.

What are the social determinants of political health? They are essential ingredients in providing citizens with a modicum of tools to exercise their political will in ways that support our democracy, to keep it healthy and sound, consistent with seeking their own best interests. They are especially relevant in a time when that democracy appears so fragile, so apparently susceptible to being bludgeoned into submission by autocrats.

These social determinants include:

A level of comfort sufficient to feel safe for the future, for the basics of food, shelter, and, not the least, gainful employment. This security blanket lessens the tendency to be angry at those that either have more, or receive support for obtaining their basic needs.

An education that promotes critical thinking. It speaks for itself when a measurable percentage of a population thinks that Sarah Palin made sense. The lack of ability to think critically is a direct result of underfunding and undermining public education, tolerating decades of incompetence that have left us with people who have not been supplied with reasonable tools to determine fact from fiction, and propaganda from self-interest.

Access to fair, unbiased news and information. Let's merge Fox and MSNBC into one station that provides at least over time, if not moment to moment, a balanced view of the world. Failing that – okay, it won't happen – require stations licensed as news stations to provide time for the expressions of other versions of the news. Allow free ad time for rebuttals. Shout loud to people that there are other points of view it wouldn't kill them to listen to.

A faith that public institutions act fairly and in your interest. It's hard not to be partisan on this. Since 1994, the Republican Party has single-mindedly promoted the interest of its supporters over the common health of the nation. They called a first-time black president "liar" in his address to Congress. They repudiate science, logic and common sense in denying climate change and supporting energy policies that enrich their donors at the expense of, well, everybody else, including their own children.

We've just seen a cabinet nomination process that was so profoundly corrupt Senators didn't seem to mind being lied to, let alone be put off by the ignorance of the people being put in charge of the machinery of government.

Which is not say that there have not been failures on the other side. In particular, Democrats and liberal organizations have gotten so engrossed in defending the rights of various minority groups – which is not to dispute, lord they sure need the help – that they have ignored the equally painful experiences of the people so left behind in a world of change, who have seized on some form of fundamentalism, whether economic, religious, or populist, to try to retain any sense of balance.

The rust belt revolt wasn't an accident, it stemmed from fatuous notions that a 55 year old out of work factory person could be reimagined as a computer programmer. And then ignoring them almost categorically. People without a baseline of comfort and security will get angry thinking that others are getting for free what they have to pay for. And they'll act out that anger by grabbing onto the shiniest rock in their swirling river. The liberal spectrum needs to support these people and ideas as much as the conservatives need to acknowledge climate change.

An ability to reflect on one's choices and decisions, and to understand that many political beliefs are based on highly personal reasons. We believe what we believe. Once we say we're an x or a y, we then go along with the x or y set of axioms, regardless of what they are and what evidence there might be to dispute them.

We think what we know is the truth, and thus the other opinion must be false, held by people who are thus bad, and down we go, never stopping for a second to think that they are in the same perceptual state. It's like blaming a visitor for not knowing you're supposed to shake with the left hand. Or thinking that if you're not into my God, then you are doomed.

An understanding that what the Constitution is often really about is what the Bible is all about: do unto others as you would have them do unto you. Let them speak, pray, hope and dream in their own ways and languages, and ask that they give you the same privilege.

There's little point at this time in trying to change anybody's mind based on a rational set of arguments. The very rational and smart columnists on the NY Times OpEd page have been making sense for years, making them among the most ignored public figures around. Rather than chip at the iceberg's tip, we need to go deeper, to address the social determinants of political health to create a process that will organically lead to a more balanced social and cultural structure.

Absent that process, we will continue to just treat the skin of our political system while its organs decay.

A friend and I manage to talk our way past various checkpoints, all the way to ground zero. Why do I so want to get there? It is not for prurient curiosity, I am sure of this. It is more – this is my home, my city.

As we walk, I hear myself muttering, "Oh God, Oh God," the sound fetid under my air mask. Seven WTC looks like the compressed mass that could become a black hole, pancaked concrete and steel of unimaginable density, the largest pile of rubble above ground that can be seen. We get to in front of the Plaza which opened on to the buildings. Four and Five WTC, which flanked the entrance, are both black and rust-brown charred hulks. All the glass is gone, they are charred husks. Four has a V-shape staved in at its southern end, whether from debris or collapse we cannot tell. The street ends in a ten story lattice work of steel, thrown from the upper levels of presumably the south tower, embedded in the ground like a giant knife. It's crisscross pattern looks like the sugared top of a cake. As far north as we can see, an unending stream of trucks, people and material pour towards the site; I wonder how it can keep absorbing it all.

This is New York City? 2001?

Liberals Barbecue Too

October, 2018

> *Liberals and conservatives could find common ground in their shared acknowledgement that relationships formed around more than property – built around family, friends, children, parents, colleagues and compatriots – are vitally significant to a satisfying, well-lived life*

A strain of purported conservative columnists, pundits and politicians feed their followers a storyline equating liberals with godless, acommunal hedonists, and accuse everyone left of center with perpetuating a Sixties lifestyle and philosophy of self-indulgence.

None of it is true, but it resonates well with those aggrieved by contemporary challenges.

I run in circles that conservatives would consider unabashedly liberal: former public defenders, a senior ACLU official, technologists, generally well-educated (some even Ivy League!), not rich but financially secure. Members of the so-called liberal elite. Even worse, as baby boomers we are further derided by the right as self-centered, lacking a moral center.

As for being self-centered, most of us have worked 60 hours a week and more for our entire lives, often in the service of others. We've raised wonderful children, many of whom also now work on behalf of others. We've conducted our personal and professional lives with integrity and compassion. And when we gather around our tribal touchstones—including, yes, barbecues—we argue, agree, and frequently agree to disagree. Like most Americans, we seek the bonds and comforts of community.

By community, I don't mean the aspirational conservative community of the country club, insulated and homogenous, reflecting the conservative's instinctive response to change and challenge: to build a wall, literal or figurative, when information doesn't support their views, no matter how anachronistic. Sweating in Mar a Lago while denying climate change.

In contrast, the liberal community is a mixed neighborhood, diverse and heterogeneous. It can be messy, since its contrasts make it harder to manage or find consensus. This openness has been the liberals' undoing, rendering them vulnerable to the withering and relentless, take-no-prisoners, dismiss-the-Other assaults launched for decades by the likes of Gingrich, the Koch Brothers, and their ilk.

The heat of these assaults has evaporated the quality of empathy from American public life: devoured by radical self-interest, lit by those exploiting fears to keep their privileges intact, using as fuel perceived and concocted threats to social status and structure. Loudly claiming independence and liberty for themselves they freely deny others.

Self-described conservatives choose to conflate liberalism with a distorted view of the Sixties, attacking in one stroke two threads which challenged their entrenched social and political hierarchies of status and wealth. Why did so many women support Trump in 2016, and back Kavanaugh in 2018? Much as antebellum plantation women abided the horrors of slavery, it is to preserve their way of life and sense of position, considerations which override matters of decency and gender.

Today's conservatives create and milk feelings of being threatened and ignored, to ignite their followers to become affronted by a perceived lack of status, and build a sense that liberals do not care about them nearly as much as they care about those marginalized by race, gender or sexual orientation — the very populations that conservatives target who thus need support. Lindsey Graham's outburst during the Kavanaugh hearing had nothing to do with appropriateness issues but was calculated to play to the emotions of those who feel besieged. In Graham's performance, the theater of ideology masked the actors' self-interest.

The very labels "conservative" and "liberal" bear scant relevance to the nation's political dynamics. Put simply: there are people who care only about the people they know and those that look like them; and there are people who care about others, even if they look different and speak in foreign tongues.

There's a reason cities and towns that have succeeded in revitalizing themselves are called "progressive." They don't cling to a past that cannot be restored, if it ever actually existed; they seek to share wealth instead of concentrating it; they don't sacrifice equitable treatment for all to maintain a powerful few. They recognize market forces and leverage them, instead of clinging to myths of bygone structures as if they were future opportunities. They welcome the energy and creativity of today's youth and embrace the concurrent challenges they offer. They think solar, not coal. They solve problems based on pragmatic realities, not ideologies.

The Sixties was an era that didn't just seek different answers, it asked different questions, most notably, how to find meaning in life that wasn't simply material. Those of us who were active in the Sixties sought self-expression that wasn't merely a hedonistic escape into self-indulgence. It was a search for alternative values, in particular values that respected others; it combined public political action with an ethical underpinning that was directed at improving the lot of others. The comparison to the energies unleashed at a Trump rally is stark.

Like today's liberals, Sixties activism prized a society that offers genuine opportunity for all − for economic advancement, for self-expression, for dominion over one's own body. We didn't try to impose our values on others by force, and we never attempted to deny others the rights of citizenship or the dignity of humanity.

The Sixties liberal response to convulsive times was to question authority; today's conservatives response to convulsive times renders democracy easy prey to authoritarianism. In their need to find clear, unambiguous guidance they open the door to power that exploits fears rather than challenges them. They nurture Trump in creating a toxic resonance frequency between the message and the audience, rallies whose voices feed off each other, equating truth with volume.

The pervasive efforts by Trump and his enablers to disconnect liberal beliefs from any sense of community values serves their purpose of creating a wedge to separate voters from their own self-interest, to drive them away from candidates who seek greater social and economic equity for the very people who are led to disdain them.

That division engenders a national tragedy. For liberals and conservatives could find common ground in their shared acknowledgement that relationships formed around more than property – built around family, friends, children, parents, colleagues and compatriots – are vitally significant to a satisfying, well-lived life. But only if they can refrain from trying to impose their moral constraints on how those relationships should be constructed. Live and let live contains a primordial wisdom, along with do unto others.

One of the most influential figures guiding Sixties cultural evolution was Gandhi, and his precept that no side has a monopoly on the truth. Contrast that to the certainty that promotes value judgments based on moral superiority, and the willingness by conservatives to impose those judgments, in making war, in allowing guns everywhere to everybody, in defying women's rights. All the while fattening bank accounts at the expense of those being led by their faith in those judgments.

Many who shroud themselves in the cloak of conservatism, selectively quoting Bible and Constitution, do so primarily to serve their own self-interests, economic power and moral impositions. Liberals, our families, our friends, those who live for others as well as themselves, have values just as powerful as those who attack them. We enjoy communities, we sing in choirs, we work pro bono. And we gather around the barbecue.

So, how would you like your steak?

These great buildings, I think, these magnificent creatures. They absorbed a shock that would have toppled any other building immediately. Even as they were wounded and dying, they stood, stood long enough to let thousands escape, protecting their own to the last, until even their massive strength buckled under the onslaught. In their last moments I could see the fires burning behind the steel girders, into empty space, almost like when the buildings were first built and the interiors unfinished. They gave to us their last full measure, protracting as long as they could the moment when shock and heat, fire and hate crumpled them to the ground. Like all New Yorkers I have a favorite picture of them, lit as red slivers in sunset coming back on Amtrak from Washington, or on the turnpike, the first indications of being close to home.

Of course they were a symbol. And no matter how many such icons may be attacked, the deep spirit that built them will never be hit, much less destroyed.

It is, let's face it, perversely thrilling and solidifying to be in the grip of something so much larger. I am reminded of college readings of existentialists who said they only found personal meaning in the midst of World War II. In an age incessantly in search of identity, we are having one handed to us.

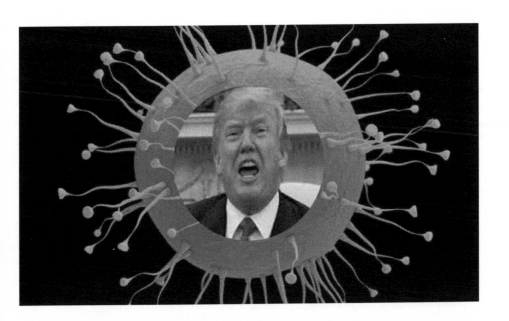

Trump: Virus or Vaccine

February 2019

Perhaps this was a form of inoculation, a mild case to avoid the fatal one

There's a Buddhist saying, "turn poison into medicine." Our local version is "turn lemons into lemonade."

There's no doubt many view Trump as a poison injected into the arteries and lifeblood of our nation, of the democratic institutions and norms we hold dear, of the Constitutional protections we cherish.

But just as a vaccine works by injecting a bit of the bad stuff into our system to help us build up the ability to control it and not be overwhelmed by the disease, so perhaps Trump has unwittingly (for there is no wit in him) provided us with the same beneficial service.

America's esteem in the world has declined precipitously under the Trump years. What is most troubling about that is if that decline is viewed as having implications for the very nature and survivability of democracy itself. If America, blessed with the protection of oceans and friendly borders, abundant in natural resources and a people with great historic energy and creativity, can be so threatened, what does that mean for other nations?

But perhaps the opposite lesson can be drawn. We have had the poison of autocracy, of arrogant self-serving leadership, injected into our system. Other nations in these circumstances have fallen prey to the forceful imposition of such leadership, ending up with dictators, with the suppression of freedom, with the horrors of mass detention and murder. But perhaps this was a form of inoculation, a mild case to avoid the fatal one.

Think Germany, of course. Think Argentina. Think of the declines in freedom that repeatedly undermine life in Russia, that breed the Chinese autocrats. All doing very nicely for themselves while plundering others.

And now think of the so-called populist, right wing movements, engulfing Europe. The dissatisfactions that fed Brexit, that are moving Hungary, that challenge the freedoms we thought were entrenched and now appear threatened. They look at us and think, if it can happen there, then it can surely happen here.

But there's more to the story. Yes, we have venom coursing through our system. At the top, it's setting a tone that frees up hatred, racism, misogyny, that pillages all but the very rich at the expense of everyone else, that is destroying the environment piece by piece, that is setting us up for the catastrophes of climate change in order to protect the profits of companies and people that seemingly will do anything to make and have more.

Granted, it's not a pretty picture.

But the genius of the American system has been its form of inertia, that one way or another pulls back to a center. The courts, compromised as they are at the top, have been safeguards to many of the extremist positions Trump has attempted to foist on us, to feed the demagoguery that got him elected and he thinks will keep him in office. Institutions such as the ACLU have received more support and stepped up their relentless pursuit of justice, an ingredient essential to the maintenance of a free state and democracy.

The 2018 elections foretold a shift in representation as the body politic generates the antibodies promoted by the innoculation, one that is less cowed, more challenging, more concerned about the protection of the people than their exploitation. The disturbing psychopathologies that have been unleashed have spurred a pushback, demanding decency for groups that have historically been denied it. Women, people of color, are not just finding their voices, but finding listeners. It's a turbulent time, and these eddies and flows aren't conclusive.

Corruption is the biggest danger, as demonstrated in so many South American and African countries that slid into despair. And there is no doubt how pervasive the corruption is, from a President and family that seek to benefit from the office, grubbing for every penny, to the enablers around them, who abuse their offices for the enrichment of their colleagues and through lavish grotesque expenditures.

Wherever a bright light has shone on this shoddy cast of characters, it has revealed their schemes. But the question is, how much has gone undiscovered, and what illicit gains will never be revealed? Corruption erodes trust in institutions, from paying taxes to believing in equitable treatment before the law. Once gone, trust is hard to recover.

So abroad and home, one overriding question is: how much damage Trump has done is irreparable? Time allows for reconciliation, for readmission of past sinners into the fold, in sports and entertainment, but if no one pays the price, the cost is immeasurable.

We may yet drown in the virus of autocracy that Trump embodies. But we may also use it as a serum to generate the healthy counterbalances of our institutions and our people, that will right the ship and put it back on the course of democracy we originated. That outcome will have resonances for us living here, and also for the rest of the world.

They are watching.

The shredded skins of surrounding buildings — One Liberty Plaza, the Millennium Hotel — look raked, slashed by talons of steel, concrete and glass. Here, the flat abstractions of TV take on their full dimensions — the enveloping feel of the destruction, the sense of desolation, dislocation, the quiet purpose that fills tired men and overwrought machines trying to enter the void. We speak in whispers. Like the image of the buildings collapsing three days ago, it is almost impossible to relate what I see to what I hold inside. There was no continuity, just this abrupt falling off the edge of a catastrophic cliff. It will take time to reconcile what was with what is.

Behind the plaza even higher steel lattice works somehow stand. The smoke obscures any further views to the west, as if this place still wants to hold a claim on our vision. High atop the lattices sparks of iron cutting dot the sky. They will work and work and work. The dead will rise slowly. We will seek action that invites reaction. This is just the beginning.

About the Author

Robert M. Herzog is well positioned to be an astute observer of America. He's been a successful entrepreneur and pioneer in media and technology, energy and healthcare, finance and City Winery. He lived at the intersection of power and politics as Director of New York City's Energy Office, and helped develop Centers for Social Justice for a public interest group. He is a published novelist, with his "unputdownable" book *A World Between* casting a shrewd light on the way science and politics intersect. He has published numerous poems, short stories and essays, and directed an award winning short film, *Flights*. He's a Brooklyn boy who's climbed Mt. Kilimanjaro, ran big rivers, and remembers the taste of the first (and subsequent) great wine he drank. From his coming of age in the Sixties to his active involvements today, he has maintained a perspective both engaged with and detached from the world around us. This collection of essays represents sharp, often prescient commentaries on an America that is, and one that could be.

Made in the USA
Middletown, DE
17 November 2019